MH01068132

Praise for *Awesome Nightfall*

"This remarkable life and poetry of Saigyō is essential reading: essential to understanding Japanese literary tradition, and essential to understanding the role of Japan's most influential poet in the history of its Buddhism. Saigyō found beauty in the temporality of things and identified with ordinary villagers throughout his famous journeys, writing poems that remain as elegant, perceptive, and moving today as they were a thousand years ago. William R. LaFleur presents a striking portrait of the man and his work. His scholarship and artistry are commendable. *Awesome Nightfall* is a classic."—Sam Hamill, author of *Dumb Luck*

"Extraordinary. This fascinating work is equal parts biography, history, poetry, and even mystery as it traces the life and mind of an elusive and complex figure of Japanese culture. This book is one of the rare works that leaves the reader overflowing with satisfaction in knowing something important and wonderful was achieved in the trip through its pages."—*New York Resident*

"In 1140, Saigyō cast off his warrior past and entered his poetic and priestly vocation. Attached to no monastery, he roamed Japan, engaging in religious austerities and honing his skills. William R. LaFleur's *Awesome Nightfall* offers us a more complex, more human Saigyō—reclusive, yes, but still a very close observer of his times, viewing the enveloping darkness from the heights 'where none can view me / but I can review all things.'"—*The Asahi Shimbun*

"A beautifully proportioned work of lucid scholarship and superb literary translation. This fruit of LaFleur's long and inspired labor not only honors the great Buddhist poet Saigyō, but the intelligence and heart of readers as well."—Mike O'Connor, translator of *The Clouds Should Know Me By Now* and *Where the World Does Not Follow*

"Bill LaFleur's translations of Saigyō's poetry have opened up a window on twelfth-century Japan, providing us with firsthand glimpses of the Buddhist religion, the valuation of nature, and the specific spirit of the times."—Mircea Eliade

"Saigyō lived in twelfth-century Japan, but from reading his poetry, it doesn't feel like it. The first half of *Awesome Nightfall* is an account of his life in the turbulent Japanese culture amid which he was raised. Dotted with his poems, it provides a good ground from which to read the second half, which consists of about 150 *waka* (traditional five-line poems). His poems are alive to the vivid transformations of inner and outer worlds. This is an inspiring volume, poetically and spiritually."—*Dharma Life*

"A quarter of a century ago, LaFleur published his book on Saigyō, *Mirror for the Moon*, which *Awesome Nightfall* thoughtfully and masterfully supersedes. LaFleur sketches Saigyō's life in bold strokes and introduces new findings for the English-reading audience. The book opens up fascinating and important questions, and as such this volume will be an interesting choice for seminars on Japanese medieval literature, history, or religion."—*Philosophy East & West*

Awesome Nightfall

Awesome Nightfall

THE LIFE, TIMES, AND POETRY

OF SAIGYŌ

William R. LaFleur

Wisdom Publications • Boston

Wisdom Publications
199 Elm Street
Somerville MA 02144 USA
www.wisdompubs.org

©2003 William R. LaFleur

All rights reserved.
No part of this book may be reproduced in any form or by any means, electronic or
mechanical, including photography, recording, or by any information storage and retrieval
system or technologies now known or later developed, without the permission in writing
from the publisher.

Library of Congress Cataloging-in-Publication Data
LaFleur, William R.
    Awesome nightfall : the life, times, and poetry of Saigyō / William R. LaFleur.
      p.   cm.
    Includes bibliographical references and index.
    ISBN 0-86171-322-2 (pbk. : alk. paper)
      1. Saigyō, 1118–1190. I. Saigyō, 1118–1190. Poems. English & Japanese. Selec-
tions. II. Title.
    PL788.5.Z5 L34 2002
    895.6'14—dc21   2002151801

07 06
5   4   3   2

Cover image: Kayama Matazo, "Flowers" (1978). From the collection of The National
    Museum of Modern Art, Tokyo.
Cover by Anna Herrick/TLrggms
Interior by Gopa & Ted2

Wisdom Publications' books are printed on acid-free paper and meet the guidelines for
permanence and durability of the Committee on Production Guidelines for Book
Longevity of the Council on Library Resources.

Printed in United States of America.

This book was produced with environmental mindfulness. We have elected to print
this title on 50% PCW recycled paper. As a result, we have saved the following
resources: 11 trees, 7 million BTUs of energy, 946 lbs. of greenhouse gases, 3,927 gallons
of water, and 504 lbs. of solid waste. For more information, please visit our web site,
www.wisdompubs.org

This is the book I promised
to Mariko and Kiyomi,
who now have it along with my thanks to them.

Contents

Preface

"FREE AND EASY WANDERING" designates an appealing way of life according to *Chuang tzu,* but it is, in fact, a path that few have entered either freely or easily. Saigyō's life was too difficult to be so designated, even though it included several extended journeys. After he died, his contemporaries praised him for having shown that the life of a Buddhist monk can be fully compatible with a dedication to writing poetry. Proving this, however, involved a lifelong, often painful, struggle. The real Saigyō was not quite as reclusive as later portraits made him out to be. He lived in horrific times and could not easily tear his attention away from what was going on. And he obviously struggled with internal demons—related to sex, to worries about the karmic imprint of his warrior past, to anxiety about loss of social visibility through taking the tonsure, and to certain items he successfully kept concealed from all later generations.

Pithy phrases that fused the "way of poetry" with "the Way of Buddha" were common in twelfth-century Japan and had a certain caché. But Saigyō realized that to test their validity required putting the whole of a life into the experiment—and with an outcome far from certain. And he knew it had to be a life intentionally disconnected from the lives of contemporaries, friends, even lovers—that is, persons who, even though themselves poets, were not engaged in precisely *this* experiment.

Thirty years ago, when I was just beginning to study this poet, there was a perceptible dry spell within Japanese scholarship on Saigyō. The idealized image of this poet had cracked, but there was little yet to take its place. The principal students of Japanese literature in North America were cold-shouldering him. My mentor at the University of Chicago, the late Joseph M. Kitagawa, however, maintained that study of this twelfth-century monk could be as fine an aperture into medieval Japanese Buddhism as one might find. And then Masao Abe, a philosopher of Zen, graciously introduced me to the late Professor Kitayama Masamichi, a student of Western literature who also had a profound grasp of medieval Japanese poetry. Reading and analyzing poem after poem together with Kiyatama, he genially badgered me. He was critical of what he had read in translation. "People both in Japan and in the West want a sweetened Saigyō," he claimed and then went on to point out that Saigyō had a difficult life, lived through tempestuous times, and fought hard to find the exact nexus between Buddhism and poetry. More importantly, he insisted, even today's Japanese readers, modern in their tastes, easily forget that Saigyō lived in a medieval episteme in which the claims of Buddhism were not to be taken lightly. If, in fact, the way of poetry were ultimately *not* compatible with his vows as a monk, Saigyō assumed that he had thrown more than this one, present life into jeopardy. He took the risks as real.

In 1978 I published *Mirror for the Moon: A Selection of Poems by Saigyō (1118–1190)*, and, although well received, it strikes me now as a somewhat "sweeter" Saigyō than the one I have come to know and will try to represent here in *Awesome Nightfall*. A large factor in this difference is that the present book relates the poems to a fairly extensive account of the poet's life. This is in part because Japanese scholarship on Saigyō has in recent decades not only provided much more detail about that life, but has, almost without exception, insisted that it is impossible to understand the specificity and beauty of Saigyō's verse unless his commitment to the Buddhist path, often explicit but always implicit, is taken seriously. Now fortunately translated into English, the third volume of a history of Japanese literature by Jin'ichi Konishi, probably the twentieth century's master scholar of that literature, makes this point about Saigyō abundantly clear. Readers of the present book may wish to compare my translations with the usually much more crisp and lean renderings of Saigyō by Burton Watson in his *Poems of a Mountain Home*.

Hoping to give the general reader unencumbered access to this portion of the Saigyō trove, I have put references and discussions of interest to specialists into pages at the book's end, citing the page number and calling out the relevant passage. Because it incorporates poems by Saigyō found in the *Kikigaki-shū* and other sources and, moreover, does so in a conveniently numbered fashion, the Nihon koten zensho edition of the *Sanka-shū* edited by Itō Yoshio has been the edition I have followed. The number provided after the romanized version of each poem is in accord with that sequence. When a second number appears in brackets that is because the same poem or a variant form of it was selected for inclusion in an imperial collection, the *Shinkokin-shū*. The *Saigyō zen-shū* edited by Kubota Jun is a twelve-hundred-page treasury of variant Saigyō texts, prose items that he possibly authored, and works such as Noh plays built on his poetry that show how later ages honored him. Kubota's work is a model we too should strive to someday imitate in this domain. Exactly why I have given this book the title I have will, I hope, become clear to the reader who goes with it all the way.

Poems here that originally appeared in *Mirror for the Moon* were greatly benefited by discussions of them with Gary Snyder. Thanks to an invitation from Koyama Hiroshi, I was able to spend a very profitable half year in 1990 at the Kokubungaku Shiryōkan in Tokyo, updating my own studies of Saigyō through contact with the preeminent scholars of this topic. Their work benefited me immensely. My debt to Matsuno Yōichi and Komine Kazuaki is especially large. Fruitful discussions of religion and literature in Japan with Richard Gardner have been a constant over the years. Students and colleagues both at UCLA and the University of Pennsylvania have added much to the making of this book. I am grateful to David Kittelstrom for his enthusiasm for this project and his exemplary editing. Kayama Matazo and the National Museum of Modern Art in Tokyo graciously permitted use of his superb painting for the cover. And to Mariko and Kiyomi, who at times may have thought I too must have left the householder's life (or at least its duties) in order to work on Saigyō, I express my deepest thanks of all.

Selected Places of Importance in Saigyō's Life

1. Heian (today's Kyoto)
2. Mount Yoshino
3. Mount Kōya
4. Ise
5. Sanuki Province (in Shikoku)
6. Bizen Province
7. Shirakawa Barrier
8. Mount Ōmine
9. Ōwada (today's Kobe)
10. Nara
11. Saya-no-nakayama
12. Eguchi (in today's Osaka)
13. Mount Fuji
14. Kamakura
15. Hiraizumi

JAPAN

The Life and Times of Saigyō

T{RULY FINE POETRY} sits uncomfortably under any label. Yet, as long as qualifiers do not overwhelm what is universal in the poetry to which they have been attached, they can have value. To forbid any reference to Dante or Milton as "Christian poets" would be to deny something of central importance in the sensibilities and writing of both men. And in a similar fashion we may refer to Saigyō as Japan's foremost "Buddhist" poet—and do so without short-changing what is universal in his verse.

What is best in his poetry, however, avoids the pious platitude. Much of the time Saigyō, originally a samurai, grappled with the implications of having become a monk. And, because he lived in "interesting" times, he struggled to understand and articulate the connection between his religious tradition and the social chaos he witnessed firsthand. Rightly known to many Japanese today as an unusually perceptive celebrant of nature's beauty, Saigyō's sensitivity toward human conflict was equally deep. War was much on his mind. And he wrote about it more than any other poet of his era.

Bashō, Japan's best-known poet, explicitly named Saigyō, who lived four centuries earlier, as the poet of the past to whom he was most indebted. And that debt is implicit in his writings, both prose and poetry. Yet there are real differences. There is something detectably modern in Bashō, whereas Saigyō's view of reality is clearly medieval. Perhaps because he was not as proximate a witness of man's inhumanity to man, Bashō would not have written about Buddhist hells in the way that Saigyō did. And, whereas Saigyō shows an existential anxiety about ways in which his multiple passions were locked in a struggle with his vows as a monk, Bashō traveled dressed in borrowed clerical robes, wore them lightly, and jested about being the equivalent of a bat, not clearly one thing or another.

I agree with those Japanese scholars of this subject who insist that any adequate grasp of Saigyō and his work requires attention to his life and his personal interaction with events of his time. And it appears that Saigyō himself wanted his poetry to be seen in this way. That is why, to a degree not seen in any other poet of his time, he prefaced many of his verses with prose introductions that located his writing in time, space, and occasion. This is not to deny that he, like others, could assume a fictive posture at times. It is merely to underscore something noted by Brower and Miner more than forty years ago—namely, that Saigyō allowed less "aesthetic distance" between himself and the persona of his verse than did his contemporaries.

In the year 1140, in an unnamed temple in or near Heian, the older name for today's Kyoto, Saigyō became a tonsured monk. He was twenty-three years old. And it was a move that surprised, even startled, his contemporaries. From that point on, consorting with other monks proved an important, although far from exclusive, part of his life. Razoring the head to a bald pate, at least in this man's case, literally embodied a decision to cease being a warrior and to enter into the path of the Buddhist life. It shaped almost everything he did and wrote for the remaining half century of his lifespan. A struggle within himself to relate *events*—large social ones as well as the more private ones of his own life—to the question of what it might mean to be a Buddhist was central to him. That struggle, consequently, is part of many of the more than two thousand poems of his we have.

The majority of these verses cannot be dated with any accuracy. But, as just noted, he affixed informative prose headnotes to many. Equally interesting, however, were those episodes in his own life about which he registers personal pain but leaves in tantalizing obscurity. And since these events clearly figured into his own struggle to understand what it might mean for him to follow the vocation of a Buddhist monk, in this book I employ and follow those Japanese scholars who have used a variety of resources to try to figure out what facts may have lain behind those portions of Saigyō's life he seems to have wanted to leave concealed.

The nature of his death, discussed at its appropriate place in the chronology here, left such an impression on his contemporaries that soon afterward hagiographic accounts of his life and death appeared. These were pious romanticizations that filled in the informational lacunae with invented materials assimilating his life story to that of Shakyamuni Buddha. This meant that throughout the medieval period and until the twentieth century, the general image of this poet-monk was that of a supremely enlightened person. Needless to say, modern scholarship has shown that reality was far more complex—and also much more interesting. What we now tend to find importantly "Buddhist" in his life and verse has more to do with his finely sharpened sense of the world's *samsara* than with any clear sense of him as having lived long in some state of continuous *nirvana*.

One felicitous byproduct of the collapse of the romanticized version has been a renewed appreciation of his poetry. The poems, with very rare exceptions, are all in the form referred to by Japanese as *waka,* the most basic form of their tradition and slightly longer than what came into being later, namely, the *haiku.* The *waka* usually had thirty-one syllables in a 5-7-5-7-7 sequence, although Saigyō, more often than other poets, stretched this "rule" by throwing in an extra syllable from time to time. Of course, the lavish employment of homonyms in traditional Japanese poetry meant that whole phrases and sometimes whole poems could have more than one reading or signification. *Engo,* or words with meanings associated with words found elsewhere in a given *waka,* allow for more significations and fullness than may first appear. It may be said that in this verse form—as in other aspects of their cultural life—the people of Japan have shown an extraordinary skill in careful packaging. The *waka* too is best opened with care, close attention, and appreciation for the skill of the person who put so much into so small a container.

To provide details of what is known about Saigyō's origins and early life involves noticing that early on—that is, until he became a monk and took on names with Buddhist significations, eventuating in "Saigyō"—his still-secular name identified him as being from the Satō branch of the vast Fujiwara clan. His personalized tag was Norikiyo. Of great significance for understanding both the biography and the verse of Saigyō is the fact that the Satō was a military house, one claiming descent from Fujiwara Hidesato. Hidesato was a warrior who in 940 had been instrumental in suppressing a revolt against imperial authority in northeastern Japan, had himself probably killed the leader of that uprising, and was subsequently celebrated for his courage and skills. Memory of him remained strong. Two hundred years or nine generations later, Norikiyo clearly grew up in a family that made much of its own long service to the imperial house. His paternal great-grandfather had probably been the one who moved the family more-or-less permanently to the capital of Heian, although the family's roots and many of its continuing connections were in the northeastern area of Japan's principal island.

In a poem written near the end of his life, Saigyō appears to bring forward memory of his—that is, Norikiyo's—childhood and an early fascination with aspects of the warrior's life.

> *shino tamete*
> *suzume yumi haru*
> *o no warawa*
> *hitai eboshi no*
> *hoshige naru kana*   1812

> Toy bamboo bow
> in hand, a mere child takes
> aim at a sparrow
> and already longs to wear
> a warrior's headgear.

Kubota Jun, the leading Saigyō scholar today, sees the poet here recognizing how, early in his life, he wanted not only to follow the family tradition by becoming a samurai, but wished to gain a high level of skill in the use of the bow and arrow. His specific dream, later realized, had been to take part in the contests known as *yabusame,* in which archers mounted on horses shoot arrows at a sequence of targets while galloping at breakneck speeds. Public exhibitions of such skills were held in Saigyō's time within the precincts of Shinto shrines. The level of equestrian skill required was very high, and, importantly, he wrote precisely about his horsemanship in what is probably his earliest extant poem.

> *fushimi suginu*
> *oka-no-ya ni nao*

todomaraji
hino made yukite
koma kokoromin

Taking off from Fushimi,
galloping nonstop over
Oka-no-ya's hills,
I spur him on to Hino to test
what this young horse can do!

Norikiyo's physical prowess extended also to the court sport of the times, *kemari*. This game, probably an import from China, had been popular among the Japanese nobility since the seventh century and involved trying to kick a deerskin ball so that it would remain aloft as long as possible. Fujiwara Yorisuke, who wrote up a record of this sport, noted at the time that Norikiyo "was highly regarded for his exceptional ability in *kemari*."

Although Saigyō's family was later referred to as a "family of wealth," its *social* position in the capital was not equal to that of the court nobility. Rather, once they had moved to the capital, the Satō people, hereditary warriors, functioned as guards for royal persons and had official commissions as such. Norikiyo's father, Yasukiyo, was temporarily relieved of his commission, perhaps because of some minor infraction of the rules or decorum. His name drops out of all records by the time Norikiyo is only three years old, and it seems quite likely that he died at a relatively young age.

This did not effect Norikiyo's career for long. Although a request for advancement made at age fifteen was not accepted, by eighteen he had become a captain of the imperial guard. Most important for his career was the close link he forged with members of the Tokudaiji family, a different sub-branch of the Fujiwara, but, unlike the Satō, one much closer to the imperial family. Some key members of the Tokudaiji served among the highest ministers of state. Norikiyo during his teen years became a retainer of Tokudaiji Saneyoshi (1095–1157). Very important for multiple reasons—and many that impacted upon Saigyō's career and poetry—was the fact that Saneyoshi's younger sister Shōshi (1101–45), celebrated for her extraordinary beauty, became the principal empress consort to Emperor Toba (1103–56, r. 1107–23) and the mother of two later emperors, Sutoku and Go-Shirakawa.

Saneyoshi's close connections to the throne meant that his retainer, the young Norikiyo, also gained access—such access as could be given to a warrior whose status did not equal that of Saneyoshi and his family. Norikiyo at some point became a member of an elite corps of court-based samurai, the North-Facing Warriors, a band of men officially charged with the defense of persons who, having been emperors in their youth, had "retired" while still young and then remained in "retirement" palaces for many decades. Through his connections Norikiyo got to serve in the retirement palace not only of Toba but also, later, in that of his successor, Sutoku (1119–64).

We get a unique glimpse of Norikiyo's life during this period through a poem in which he records his elation at being invited by a contemporary to write a poem on an official occasion. Norikiyo, as became his practice later when he became Saigyō, provided an informative prose introduction.

> While Fujiwara Munesuke was Middle Counselor, he presented a large number of chrysanthemums as a gift to Retired Emperor Toba. When planted, they filled the area of the eastern garden of Toba's southern palace. Kinshige, a captain of the imperial guard, invited a number of people to write verses celebrating these chrysanthemums, and I was pleased to be included among those asked:

> *kimi ga sumu*
> *yado no tsubo o ba*
> *kiku zo kazaru*
> *hijiri no miya to*
> *iubekaruran*   510

> Chrysanthemums fill
> the garden where the days are passed
> by Your Majesty—
> so "Grotto of the Holy Sage,"
> the palace name, fits very well.

There is nothing spectacular about the poem. It is formal and written on an occasion when formality was expected. He records his pleasure at being invited to provide a poem in spite of not being the social equal of the others. And since it is someone named "Kinshige" who is smoothing the way for Norikiyo to submit a poem among this elite group, it is worth nothing that Kinshige was a nephew of Saneyoshi and also someone in the Tokudaiji household. We can surmise that within the Tokudaiji household Norikiyo had been honing his own poetic skills, and that these had been gaining respect and praise—so much so that he was pushed forward to write something for the fete to honor Emperor's Toba's "retirement."

There is an important reason why I have placed scare quotes around the term "retirement." It refers not so much to an emperor's relinquishment of power but, paradoxically, to his *gaining enhanced power*. The mechanism for achieving this was an institution, largely of the twelfth century, called *insei*, or "governing while retired." Its creation made this period of time unusual in Japan's history. For more than two centuries prior to the *insei* invention, the emperors of Japan had had next to no power. This was because all decisions of significance were then being made by the senior males of the northern branch of the Fujiwara family. During the heyday of Fujiwara dominance emperors were most often enthroned at a tender age—some as young as six, many in their early teens—and abdicated often within a decade or so. These relatively young and still vulnerable persons, having Fujiwara mothers and married usually to Fujiwara women while young, were under intense and irresistable pressure to rubber-stamp decisions already made by the senior Fujiwara males. This leverage exerted on them very often included the demand that they abdicate early and live out the rest of their lives in comfortable but politically impotent retirement.

This changed during the eleventh century when Emperor Go-Sanjō (r. 1068–73) and especially his son, Emperor Shirakawa (r. 1073–87), took advantage of their relatively looser entrapment in the Fujiwara mode to turn their own retirement years into ones of *real* power. Shirakawa, whose postabdication life went on for forty-two years, was a strong-willed man with a wide gambit of operations. He provided the prototype that others strove to emulate during the twelfth century. The locus of operations of these two and all later *insei* figures was a kind of private cloister, although such places were anything but quiet or remote. Even when such "retiring" emperors took the tonsure and became in some sense royal Buddhist monks, their involvement in directing the political and social order of the so-called "secular" world was extensive. Their cloisters were, even if not the palace per se, the loci of actual power. Administrative offices were staffed and maintained there, and they were often sites of large social and artistic events. The previously cited poem of Norikiyo follows the public lie, namely that Emperor Toba in retirement was living in a building named as if it were the obscure hideaway of a Taoist recluse. The gap between the name and reality, however, was considerable. Toba's "grotto" was furnished for living on a lavish scale. And if the word "palace" designates the real locus of royal power, then these cloisters were the period's true palaces. Conversely the "palace," where lived a very young and soon-to-be retired emperor, was, at least as a place of power, no palace at all.

In the translations below we will see our poet, both in his Norikiyo phase and then later as Saigyō, moved to write about paradoxes, about gaps between reality and appearance, and about attitudes and actions that ordinary society cannot comprehend because of its own attachment to illusions. This may have arisen in part from his recognition that at society's very top—that is, in the imperial sphere—things were a hall of mirrors. Men within it could grab increased power for themselves only by acts that, on their surface, purported to be the relinquishment of power. And by serving as a guard in the "palace" of Toba and then later in that of Sutoku, Norikiyo got to see firsthand not only the activities but the contradictions in how things were articulated, structured, and run at the social and political apex of his society. It was a component of what impelled him to investigate and practice Buddhism.

Recent studies have uncovered details concerning what Norikiyo likely witnessed and experienced. They flesh out what it would have meant for him to detect contradictions in the courtly society of his era. Specifically, data have been compiled showing that the band of North-Facing Warriors, the elite band of warriors he joined, was composed of young men whose physical beauty was a requirement for their selection. This corps, brought into being by Shirakawa and employed continuously by the *insei* emperors, was responsible for providing these royal persons not only with safety but also with pleasure. Scholars have uncovered references both to "special tasks" required of these warriors and to descriptions of some individuals among them as having been the "paramours" of their royal patrons.

"Within the hidden side of the culture of the court during the *insei* period males having sex with other males was very much in vogue," wrote the late Mezaki Tokue, a historian who, more than any other, coordinated the poetry of Saigyō with data from diaries and historical records of that period. These records name individuals who were erotically involved with the retired emperors, Toba and Go-Shirakawa (1127–92) most especially. Gomi Fumihiko, perhaps the most important historian of this period, traces connections between individuals involved in these homoerotic activities, jealousies and conflicts that arose among them, and the society-shaking eruptions of violence in the capital in 1156 and 1159. He insists that these relationships had a strong but hitherto unrecognized impact upon the political and social history of the era.

Toba was the first of two retired emperors served by Norikiyo, and it is the name of Toba that shows up most frequently among the *insei* figures involved with male paramours. Among those mentioned was one of the younger men of the Tokudaiji family, Kin'yoshi, who was the same age as Norikiyo and a close associate of his. Since the sources of the time reveal these details with the implication that those involved had been making efforts to keep them hidden, we see that homosexual sex was considered irregular and out of step with the heterosexual norm of that era. This meant also that what was going on in the palaces of the *insei* emperors, however much "in vogue" privately, was not publicly condoned.

Japan in this period was hardly puritan. Multiple affairs, as celebrated through the philandering hero of the eleventh-century *Tale of Genji* and as described as the de facto situation of her own life by Sei Shonagon in her *Pillow Book,* were condoned among those who could afford them. "Nightcrawling" by men to the apartments of women was *de rigueur.* Mezaki writes:

Erotic love between males and females had from earlier times provided the most popular source for the writing of *waka* poetry. Among the courtiers eros and its pursuit were not brought under moral censure. On the contrary, [constantly changing liaisons] were thought to illustrate the [quasi Buddhist] notion of *mono no aware*. Even among monks engaged in the arts, to celebrate such love in verse was thought to pose no problem whatsoever to spiritual aspirations. And the expression of this freely in verse is something we find in a very large number of Saigyō's poems.

By contrast, the love of one male for another male involved consorting in secret and away from the public eye. Such sex had no cultural value and was socially sterile.

Mezaki asks, should we not surmise that at least one of the things prompting Norikiyo to consider becoming a monk was a sense of finding the expectations placed on him as a member of the North-Facing Warrior group distasteful, even a source of personal suffering?

The following poem, written likely just before Norikiyo became a monk, oscillates interestingly between the future and the past. It displays, however obliquely, an insight by Norikiyo into what was happening, and his interest appears to have been in communicating something of his own situation within Toba's *insei* palace.

> *iza saraba*
> *sakari omou mo*
> *hodo mo araji*
> *hakoya ga mine no*
> *hana ni mutsureshi*   1594

> When facing crises,
> what will be gone completely are
> thoughts of their perfect beauty—
> that of blossoms known intimately
> in the sage emperor's palace.

The term *hakoya,* derived from the *Chuang tzu,* was a term for a hermit sage's refuge in mountains. In Norikiyo's day it had rather recently come to refer to the palace of the retired emperor. Kubota notes that the hasty reader may think the phrase "will be gone completely" characterizes "blossoms," thus indicating their well-known ephemerality, expressed in much hackneyed verse. The grammar insists, however, that what "will be gone completely" at some future date will be the thought or memories of those blossoms. That is, Norikiyo appears, while in the midst of the court, to project himself into a future in which he no longer holds the memory of the spectacular flowers of the *insei* palace (and, by extension, all the other blandishments of life there). And the "crisis" mentioned in the first line, although also referred to as an aspect of the future, may be Norikiyo's hint that he was facing such in his own relations at the imperial court.

The prose headnote to a much-admired poem of this period made an explicit connection to his thought about leaving palace life. This question, he writes, haunted him even while engaged in what should have been a totally pleasurable activity.

> During the time when I was coming to a decision about leaving secular life, I was on the Eastern Hills with a number of people, and we were writing verses expressing our sentiments about the gathering mists there. I wrote:

sora ni naru
kokoro wa haru no
kasumi nite
yo ni araji tomo
omoitatsu kana   786

A man whose mind is
one with the sky-void steps
into a spring mist
and thinks to himself he might
in fact step out of the world.

He plays here with the double entendre of one word, *sora*—which refers to the sky but connotes as well the Buddhist emptiness—and another, *yo*—which here denotes the sense of being so enclosed by mists that the physical *world* disappears before one's eyes but with the secondary sense of a leaving of the *world* of secular life. It is a rich, skillfully executed poem. And it describes Norikiyo's state of mind.

During the tenth lunar month of 1140, the twenty-three-year-old Norikiyo left the palace and became a monk. The dharma-name given him then was En'i (Level of Perfection), and some documents thereafter refer to him by this name. Although it appeared at a later point in his monastic life, the name Saigyō, meaning "Going West," came to be the popularly accepted appellation for this person, and it remains so today.

He addressed a leave-taking poem to Retired Emperor Toba, himself thirty-seven years old at the time. It is a poem relishing irony. It was probably his last poem written while still Norikiyo.

> Written when I was petitioning the *insei* Emperor Toba to grant me his permission to leave secular life:

> *oshimu tote*
> *oshimarenubeki*
> *kono yo kawa*
> *mi o sutete koso*
> *mi o mo tasukeme* 2083

> So loath to lose
> what maybe should be loathed:
> one's place in the world;
> we maybe rescue best the self
> by simply throwing it away.

Both careful thought and linguistic skill show themselves here. Norikiyo, I suggest, cleverly mirrors the manner in which the *insei* emperors themselves had gained *by giving something away.* As noted above, they grabbed real power by giving up what most people in society, under illusion on this score, probably considered society's preeminent position. They made personal capital out of their insider knowledge that reality is not what society, or "the world," thinks it to be.

Norikiyo knew that his secular master, Toba, understood how things worked at that level. But he twisted the notion of the ironic outcome in a different but at the same time more traditional direction. His employment of it was not new in that Buddhists had always held that jettisoning the world, its pleasures, and its blandishments enables one to have access to the far-preferable spiritual benefits that accrue to practice along the Buddhist path.

I think it appropriate to see a subtly phrased admonition in the poem—even though it was meant to function first as a formal request for permission. There is a clear implication that "the world" he no longer prizes includes the ambience of Toba's palace. Does he, as some critics have suggested, imply that the palace itself is a *decadent* world? His poem implies, even if it does not directly state, that relinquishing the throne as a mere tactical move to gain more political power subverted what *Buddhists* meant by retiring from the world.

Even though I suggested above that a desire to get out of what might have been a highly charged, personally painful, or even disgraceful predicament of tabooed sex in Toba's palace could have stimulated Norikiyo's decision to leave, it is important to recognize that until recently scholars in Japan focused upon a different reason. This explanation too has the ring of plausibility. It hones in on the possibility that Norikiyo had become romantically involved with a court lady whose social position was far higher than his own and that, once this liaison had been discovered, he had no option but to leave the palace. Doing so through *shukke*—literally, leaving life as a (secular) householder—was for him the most convenient option.

If such a court lady had, in fact, been part of the picture, many students of this topic consider Taikenmon-in (1101–45) to have quite likely been the person with whom Norikiyo had gotten involved. The evidence for this theory is circumstantial and has primarily three components. The first is that Taikenmon-in, referred to above as Shōshi, was the younger sister of Toku-daiji Saneyoshi. That is, she was part of the family whose male members were very close to Norikiyo, their retainer. Thus, it is assumed, the two of them would have had occasions to meet within that context in spite of the fact that he was much younger than she. Norikiyo, as noted, was born in 1118. That same year Taikenmon-in, seventeen years old and already a famous beauty, was selected by retired emperor Shirakawa to be the empress consort for his grandson, Toba, who was sixteen at that time and on the throne.

Second, her reputation for beauty was matched by one for granting sexual favors quite liberally, even well after she had become empress. Below we will note how this aspect of her life may have precipitated an armed conflict. Here we can simply note that her readiness for multiple affairs has led some to conclude that Norikiyo may have been one of her many lovers—but to his own dismay when their status differential became known. The third piece of evidence for their affair lies in the fact that Saigyō, long after becoming a monk, carried on extensive correspondence and poetry exchanges with her ladies-in-waiting, some of whom themselves were of high court rank.

Clearly these attempts to put together a puzzle are missing far too many of the most important pieces. The documentary evidence for the existence of a homoerotic culture in Toba's palace is fairly strong. But, even if this had been a factor in Norikiyo's decision, we have no way of knowing whether he found it unpalatable in principle or whether he was jilted or offended in the context of sexual activities in which he was engaged. And, since it seems clear that many of the men having sex with other men in the palace were also erotically involved with women, personal distress over some aspect of the homosexual activity does not itself rule out the possibility that Norikiyo had also fallen into an impossible situation with a lady of the court. We simply do not know.

And, it appears, we were not meant to know. Norikiyo, just as Saigyō later, wrote very informative, even detailed, prose headnotes to poems when he thought the reader deserved to know certain things. At other times, sometimes when our curiosity is most keen, he provided nothing in detail. The evidence at the edges tantalizes. That someone, of undisclosed gender, had been a part of his decision is strongly suggested in the following:

> nanigoto ni
> tsukete ka yo o ba
> itowamashi
> ukarishi hito zo
> kyō wa ureshiki   1440

> What turned me to wanting
> to break with the world-bound life?
> Maybe the one whose love

turned to loathing and who now
joins me in a different joy.

It is likely that, unless he were merely trying to hide facts out of shame, Saigyō ensconced the reasons for his decision within mystery so that his contemporaries, as well as later generations of readers, would come to see it as he wanted it to be seen: as a decision to lead a qualitatively different kind of life, one with spiritual practice at its core. Disappointments in love, jiltings, and the like can never, at least to this way of thinking, be more than catalysts. When profounder and more powerful patterns of karmic causality are assumed to be what is really at work, more proximate events, such as erotic entanglements, exploitation, and social ignominy, are viewed as superficial facilitators, not the *cause* of a decision. Being a Buddhist and in a medieval rather than a modern context, Saigyō himself would have approached the question of causality in this way.

Whether or not he was married at this time is another unknown. The *Sompi-bunmyaku,* an often-reliable record of genealogies compiled during the late fourteenth and early fifteenth centuries, lists Saigyō as having a son named Ryūshō. It is quite possible, however, that another monk by this name who was a contemporary of Saigyō's was mistakenly listed as his son. The fictive and hagiographic *Tale of Saigyō,* written probably during the thirteenth century, makes him out to have had a daughter whom he literally had to cast aside in order to become a monk. The problem with this work, however, is that, in its eagerness to form connections between Saigyō and Shakyamuni, it invents events—in this case perhaps a child who serves as obstacle to the act of leaving the householding life. Therefore, the evidence is a bit too shaky to portray Norikiyo as having had a wife and children.

Another "loud silence" claims our attention. Nowhere does this man who became a monk in 1140 tell us at which temple he was tonsured or where he took his vows. Someone in some temple accepted his request to become a monk and gave him a dharma-name, but we know nothing of the context of his vows, or of the rationale for the religious names he received. This is because neither he, nor any contemporaneous document, tell us anything.

If we can see this as an *intentional* silence, it may indicate that he included himself among those monks of his age who had no desire to live within temples or monastic compounds or to follow their daily routines. Saigyō defines himself as being among a number of monks in his time who chose to live on the periphery of temples and monasteries. They lived in small hermitages that typically could house no more than one person. Such monks would, we now know, periodically receive some food and other provisions from the temple nearby and would, to reciprocate, go at times on tours to collect money, hopefully in large rather than small amounts, from laypersons wanting to get merit thereby. To earn the right to be a monk, but not to have to live within a temple or monastery, involved a certain trade-off. Saigyō, at least late in his life, had almost certainly been on such a tour for donations, and it is likely that his unusually extensive travels throughout Japan were related to one or another project for which donations were needed.

During the first couple of years after being tonsured, Saigyō lived either on the periphery of the capital or within walking distance of it. We have poems from this period expressing worry that living on the Eastern Hills was not giving him the necessary distance from "the world." Then he went further—for instance, to Kurama, on mountains within two or three day's journey by foot from Heian. Since he left the court during the fall, it was probably during his first winter alone that he records the misery he had been feeling within the capital. He felt the impact of his decision physically.

Having made my escape from a worldy way of life, I was in the interior of Kurama at a bamboo conduit, the water of which was frozen and not flowing. Hearing from someone that this would be the state of affairs until the arrival of spring, I wrote this poem:

> *warinashiya*
> *kōru kakei no*
> *mizu yue ni*
> *omoisuteteshi*
> *haru no mataruru*
> 623

> It was bound to be:
> my vow to be unattached
> to seasons and such—
> I, who by a frozen bamboo pipe
> now wait for water, long for spring.

While we cannot ignore the possibility that he had resided within temples at one time or another, neither he or nor anyone else suggests as much. If, indeed, his family was as wealthy as one source suggests, his basic needs may have been provided for by relatives with whom he linked up during his frequent travels.

What we know of Saigyō through his poetry and the prose he wrote to accompany it forcefully indicates that he considered the core of his vocation as a Buddhist to lie in the relatively solitary life of the monk, separated not only from the secular world, but also from the world of the large temple or monastery. He was probably among those monks of the twelfth century who profoundly disliked the competition, cutthroat at times, for rank and privilege among monks within individual temples, and also between temples. Entire monasteries were at times in something close to a state of war with one another.

Physical fighting between bands of monks was anything but uncommon. Many of the larger temples kept at their disposal ruffians who, dressed in robes, could be directed to intimidate either secular officials or rival temples and shrines. But not a few of these purveyors of violence and mayhem were themselves ordained monks—in spite of the fact that carrying anything like a weapon was strictly forbidden in the monastic regulations. Conflicts between the two major monasteries of the Tendai School took an especially overt form during Norikiyo's lifetime: In 1121, three years after his birth, and then again in 1140—that is, the exact same year of his *shukke*—warrior-monks from Enryaku-ji burned Miidera Temple (Onjō-ji), its bitter rival.

Saigyō occasionally expresses his desire to leave behind the accumulated bad karma of his family's long warrior tradition. This theme becomes ever more pronounced as his life moves along. And since something of this motif probably entered into his decision to become a monk in the first place, it would naturally have seemed meaningless for him to try to find peace while living within a temple rank with internal competition and out to topple its rivals by physical force. One of his poems appears to express precisely such an awareness:

sutetaredo
kakurete sumanu
hito ni nareba

nao yo ni aru ni
nitaru narikeri   1507

To think you've thrown
the world away and then still
live unhidden is
to be like any other worldling
still dwelling in the world of men.

The correlate to this is the wealth of poems that express either the pleasure Saigyō finds in leading the reclusive life or the suffering he encounters once he really tries to do so. Japanese scholars today have disproven earlier suggestions that this was merely a literary pose, a fictional persona. Although he was not the complete recluse or constant pilgrim that some of the later hagiographies made him out to be, it seems quite clear that Saigyō spent a good deal of time in hermitages that were relatively separate from society and made journeys that, even if not constant, show him to have possibly been the most wide-ranging pilgrim of his time.

First, however, he had to extricate himself from the capital. During his time on the Eastern Hills he was still in an area where, as evinced earlier, members of the courtier class could easily go for poem-writing excursions. The temples there had monks much involved—socially, politically, and literarily—with the courtiers in the palaces and mansions not very far away. If Saigyō were still, even occasionally, meeting some of the same persons with whom he had been involved on an erotic level before having taken Buddhist vows, he no doubt sensed a contradiction, one that either then or later could have been a personal experience informing the "To think you've thrown the world away" poem.

Fujiwara Yorinaga (1120–56), whose diary, *Taiki,* is one of the most highly regarded sources for information on the period, recorded that on the fifteenth day of the third lunar month of 1142, the monk Saigyō came to visit for the purpose of sutra-copying. The text mentions that two retired emperors (Toba and Sutoku) were connected with this activity, and, since the date for this falls within a month of Empress Taikenmon-in's tonsuring and entry into the status of Buddhist nun, it is assumed that Saigyō, well known to all these people, was being brought on board for what he could do for them in his new capacity. Formerly their guard and sometime companion, he was now their priest. Taikenmon-in, who may have had a lingering illness, died within three years at age forty-five. Her relatively early death spared her the necessity of witnessing the open strife and tragedies that would befall many of these royal persons within little more than a decade.

The following poem, most (but not all) scholars agree, appears to have been composed within a couple years of Saigyō's *shukke*. It shows up after his decision to make a more clean and unambiguous break with the society and culture of the capital.

> Having separated from the world, I was at Deer-bell Mountain (Suzuka-yama) on the way to Ise:

> *suzukayama*
> *ukiyo o yoso ni*
> *furisutete*
> *ika ni nariyuku*
> *waga mi naruran*   796 [1611]

> Shaking the bell
> on this mountain, am I loosened from
> the world now?
> Can I shake my self enough
> to know what lies ahead for me?

There is an intensity in this query about the need to go strongly up against all that holds one to older, well-grooved patterns of life. Kubota finds it significant that, although this particular mountain was notorious for outlaws who would rob and terrorize travelers, Saigyō's poem focuses entirely upon the struggle with his internal demons. What threatened him, at least from his own account, was his hankering for the left-behind world, since it could easily rob him of his vocation. In many ways it would turn out to be a lifelong struggle.

Ise is not geographically very far from Mount Kōya, where Kūkai (774–835) had begun the construction of what eventually, at least by Saigyō's day, would become a large monastic complex. He, like not a few others, seems to have taken up residence in a hermitage somewhere in the precincts of Kōya. Saigyō greatly admired Kūkai, early Japan's brilliant master of multiple skills and foremost transmitter of esoteric Buddhism.

From the perspective of the capital, Kōya was very remote, and Saigyō employed this theme of remoteness as the opening line in a series of ten poems. He notes that he wrote them at Kōya and sent them to Jakunen, a monk living at that time in Ōhara. Jakunen sent ten of his own poems in response. Saigyō records that what he sees in this place differs greatly from what would be seen back in the city. Two of this set are:

> *yama fukami*
> *koke no mushiro no*
> *ue ni ite*
> *nani kokoro naku*
> *naku mashira kana*   1289

Deep in the mountains—
sitting upright on moss used
as a mat for himself,
with not a care in the world—
is a gibbering, chattering ape.

> *yama fukami*
> *kejikaki tori no*
> *oto wa sede*
> *mono osoroshiki*
> *fukurō no koe*   1291

Deep in the mountains—
no song of birds close to what
we knew at home,
just the spine-tingling hoots
of owls in the night.

In verses such as these, the poet accents the physical and social distance placed between himself and urban society.

A more rigorous practice of Buddhist regimens for both body and mind shows up in the multiple poems he wrote about being on Mount Ōmine, a site in that period for undergoing severe, often painful, disciplines. Kubota notes that these disciplines were to emulate the sufferings of beings in the three lower realms of the six-tiered Buddhist cosmology. Hauling heavy burdens up and down such mountains gave one the experience of life as an animal. Receiving only meager provisions of food provided insight into the fate of hungry ghosts. Being tongue-lashed with accounts of one's every fault and physically beaten with canes provided a taste of life in hell. Saigyō hints at the rigors of Ōmine's routes in the following:

At a place called Ants' Crossing:

> *sasa fukami*
> *kiri kosu kuki o*
> *asa tachite*
> *nabiki wazurau*
> *ari-no-towatari*   1203

> Crack-of-morning
> climb from caves in thick
> bamboo grass beyond
> the mists: body now bending along
> stark rock forms at Ants' Crossing.

Most of the poems about this place, however, celebrate the results, and these are uniformly positive. Some of Saigyō's splendid poems about the moon and the increasing clarity of his own mind seem to flow directly from the austerities undertaken at this point in his life.

On seeing the moon at the place called Shinsen on Mount Ōmine:

> *fukaki yama ni*
> *sumikeru tsuki o*

mizariseba
omoide mo naki
waga mi naramashi   1191

Passage into dark
mountains over which the moon
presides so brilliantly...
Not seeing it, I'd have missed
this passage into my own past.

tsuki sumeba
tani ni zo kumo wa
shizumumeru
mine fukiharau
kaze ni shikarete   1193

So brilliant a moon
up there that the clouds
have sunk down
into the valley, urged along
by winds sweeping the peaks.

A far more extensive kind of pilgrimage came next. At some point before
he turned thirty Saigyō journeyed to Mutsu Province in the far northeast, no
small undertaking at that time. It is estimated that if a person left the capi-
tal in the spring, he or she would reach that destination some time in
autumn. This route, at least by the time Bashō retraced the footsteps of
Saigyō, gradually became famous—in part because it was arduous. In win-
ter it was cold. Saigyō probably wintered in the area and records having seen
edifices of Hiraizumi, a small but elegant architectural transplant of capital
culture established in 1095 in the middle of the hinterlands of the far north.
Saigyō believed he had been preceded along this route a century earlier by the
monk Nōin (998–1050?), although some sources are skeptical on this point.
    On the way northward Saigyō came to one of three barriers built along

---

the road in the eighth century to prevent the aboriginal people of the north from moving south. These places had over time been given an aesthetic patina by poets stopping at them. Having been constructed by the central authorities, they represented just a bit of the culture of the capital—but in such faraway and desolate places that their mere mention called up images of acute loneliness due to *de facto* separation from the capital and its pleasures. One at which Saigyō lingered was the barrier at Shirakawa.

> I was on pilgrimage to Mutsu Province in the northeast for spiritual discipline and stopped at what had been the checkpoint at Shirakawa. Now with a dilapidated roof, the building let the moon's beam shine right inside—curiously and beautifully so. I recalled the phrase "breezes of autumn" in a poem by the monk Nōin written at this same location. It is a place replete with tokens of the past and many memories. I added my own part by writing the following poem and fastening it to a pillar on this structure.

> *shirakawa no*
> *sekiya o tsuki no*
> *moru kage wa*
> *hito no kokoro o*
> *tomuru narikeri*   1213

> The guardhouse
> at famed Shirakawa gate,
> now ruined, lets the moon
> filter in; its shaft is like
> having another staying here.

Much current interest in this poem centers around whether or not Saigyō was aware of rumors in the capital just then that Nōin may have never gone on the pilgrimage north and had composed this poem with a fictive persona while he himself was abiding in the capital.

Concerning another person of the past with a shaky reputation, Saigyō wrote the following poem with an extensive headnote:

While in the province of Mutsu I came across an unusual-looking grave mound. I asked whose it was and was told that it belonged to a middle captain of the palace guard. When I persisted in inquiring exactly who this person might have been, I was informed that it was Fujiwara Sanekata. I was deeply saddened. Even before learning the details, I had sensed the pathos in this scene of frost-shriveled pampas grass—so fragile it was almost invisible. Later, in trying to express my feelings, adequate words were almost unavailable:

kuchi mo senu
sono na bakari o
todomeokite
kareno no susuki
katami mi zo miru   872 [793]

One part of him
escaped decay—his name,
still around here like
this field's withered grass:
my view of the relic he left.

It is as if he has to drag the desired information out of his informant. Fujiwara Sanekata, who possibly had been a husband of Sei Shōnagon, the author of *The Pillow Book*, was said to have one day entered into a verbal altercation with someone else at court. Things became somewhat violent, and then Sanekata was sent off to this remote post in the far north as punishment. There he died within a few years.

Why was Saigyō so interested in this man and so moved by seeing his grave? Some sense of identification probably lay in the fact that both had been warriors who served as palace guards. But, since we know of no specific shame or punishment attached to Saigyō's name, it is probably best simply to see him here witnessing how quickly not only bodily remains but even the makings of a gravesite can disappear from the face of the earth, reflecting upon how he himself could fade away without a trace. Taking Buddhist vows did not translate easily into a mind at ease with the prospect of sinking into invisibility. Elements in a melancholy scene pile up: the poet standing motionless in front of a time- and weather-devastated grave; the fragile, almost ghostly, heads of swaying pampas grass; and what likely was an early nightfall in this more northern setting.

It is almost as if the gravity of this poem's consideration of life's transiency was coming as a personal prelude to the events that soon thereafter shook the world to which Saigyō had once been very close. The year 1156, one of tragedy for the court, becomes the next surely datable one in his life. On the second day of the seventh lunar month, the retired Emperor Toba died at age fifty-four. This, of course, was the man in whose service Saigyō, now thirty-nine, had been a warrior guard, and it was from Toba that he had received permission to become a monk. Saigyō appears to have been living at Mount Kōya then, and, upon hearing the news, he immediately went to the capital to attend the funeral rites. He also wrote a poem.

On the occasion when the remains of Retired Emperor Toba were being escorted to their place of entombment:

michi kawaru
miyuki kanashiki
koyoi kana
kagiri no tabi to
miru ni tsuketomo 854

Different from places
Your Majesty visited before!
Tonight's sad, final
journey in this world takes you
far beyond the world itself.

This death was the catalyst for a lot of change.

For twenty-seven years Toba had, in his position as senior retired emperor, been the actual wielder of power in Japan. When he vacated the throne in 1123, it was occupied by Sutoku (1119–64), who held it for nine years between the ages of four and thirteen. Sutoku then retired as well but, still a mere teenager, was relegated to the status of *junior* retired emperor and was hardly in a position to challenge or contravene any of the decisions being made by Toba. Between his own retirement in 1142 and Toba's death in 1156, Sutoku had been waiting in the wings for a taste of the power that had till then eluded him.

The relationship between Toba and Sutoku had never been good. Despite the fact that in *official* records the former had fathered the latter, there was a lot of doubt about Sutoku's real paternity. This matter was a semi-public scandal, and it affected some of the persons who had been very close to Norikiyo before he became a monk. Toba's principal consort, it needs to be remembered, was the famed Taikenmon-in, a daughter of the Tokudaiji family. A pervasive rumor in court had it that not Toba but Toba's grandfather, the retired emperor Shirakawa, had made Taikenmon-in pregnant. This gained easy credibility because everyone knew that Shirakawa, who got what he wanted while he was "retired," had adopted this young beauty as his own daughter and had effectively forced Toba to marry her, possibly to keep her close at hand for his own use. Not surprisingly, the triangulated relationship of Shirakawa, Taikenmon-in, and Toba was very strained. Given the likeliness of truth in the allegation about Shirakawa and Taikenmon-in, it is not difficult to see why Toba was less than intimate with his so-called "son" and, more importantly, unwilling to share power with him in any way.

Toba, in fact, connived to bypass Sutoku altogether. Before his death in 1156 he had arranged for the headship of the imperial family to pass down not through any child of Taikenmon-in but, rather, through the children of another consort, a woman named Bifukumon-in. He designated her son and then her grandson to constitute the genetic line of the throne and—what was even more important in this irregular era—the position of retired monarch. The animosity between Toba and Sutoku was made intense by the older man's highhanded actions.

Sutoku saw that he had one and only one chance to undo Toba's plan and that would come with the latter's death. He had already formed some valuable alliances and had been plotting what to do. Toba, ill for two months before succumbing, sensed that something was afoot and ordered warriors to guard the palace carefully. Eight days after Toba's death Sutoku and his associates gathered their troops in one location, and the next day actual battle broke out. It lasted less than a day. A palace that had been headquarters for Sutoku's effort was burned down, and things ended with clear victory for the forces opposed to him. Two days later he was found hiding out in Ninna-ji Temple and was soon thereafter placed into imperial exile in Sanuki Province on the island of Shikoku. He died there eight years later.

What had taken place in the capital during those unusual days came to be known as the Hōgen Disturbance because the year of its occurrence, 1156, was the first year in a series of years designated as "Hōgen." Its significance went far beyond the few buildings burned, warriors killed, and emperor dispatched into exile. This was because physical violence had, for the first time in centuries, broken out in rivalries for actual power in the Japanese state. Later generations were to see the Hōgen Disturbance as the prelude to a much larger war that would envelop the land within three decades and, beyond that, a period in Japanese history when samurai rather than the emperor and court ruled the land.

Was it his long-standing connection to the the family of Taikenmon-in and through her to Sutoku that led Saigyō to rush to the city to try to link up with the monarch who had lost out and was now about to be dispatched into exile? Although Sutoku had already been taken away from it, Saigyō went to Ninna-ji and wrote a poem expressing his dismay at events.

A great calamity shook society, and things in the life of Retired Emperor Sutoku underwent inconceivable change, so that he took the tonsure and moved into the north quarters of Ninna-ji Temple. I went there and met the eminent priest Kengen. The moon was bright, and I composed the following poem:

kakaru yo ni
kage mo kawarazu
sumu tsuki o
miru waga mi sae
urameshiki kana   1316

Times when unbroken
gloom is over all our world...
above which still

presides the ever-brilliant moon:
sight of it casts me down more.

Did a worry that society might be falling into chaos and barbarism prompt Saigyō to register the note of distress that follows?

> After Retired Emperor Sutoku had gone to Sanuki and not much was heard in society any longer about poetry, I wrote the following and sent it to the monk Jakunen:

> *koto no ha no*
> *nasake taetaru*
> *orifushi ni*
> *ariau mi koso*
> *kanashikarikere*　　　　　　　　　　　　　　　　　　　　1317

> Grievous fate: to find
> you've come to live at that
> juncture in time
> when gatherings of refined poets
> are a custom just become...extinct.

Perhaps Saigyō's concern here was compounded by the fact that he only recently had been receiving increased attention for his own verse. The following had been included in the *Shikawaka-shū (Verbal Flowers Collection of Waka)* that had been ordered by Sutoku. Fujiwara Akisuke, the editor, finished it in 1151. Saigyō's poem, which follows, pursues one of his favorite themes, the paradoxes and problems associated with "throwing away the world," and appeared without his name attached. Although anonymity would have been in keeping with the theme, we can nonetheless be quite sure that Saigyō would have been gratified to see his own work now being included within imperial anthologies.

> *mi o sutsuru*
> *hito wa makoto ni*
> *sutsuru ka wa*

sutenu hito koso
sutsuru narikeri 2169 [372 in *Shikawaka-shū*]

So, then, it's the one
who has thrown his self away
who is thought the loser?
But he who cannot lose self
is the one who is really lost.

Concerning this poem Kobayashi Hideo, perhaps Japan's premier literary critic in the twentieth century, wrote:

> A poem such as this is a conceptual one, looking like it borrowed the dialectal grammatical structures of Buddhist texts.... Saigyō, making the paradox in a poem such as this into a reliable source for poetry, was opening totally new territory, a place no one had entered before.

The "conceptual" dimension recognized by Kobayashi does not, however, mean that the content was alien to Saigyō's emotional experience. In fact, this and somewhat similar poems of the time bring to the surface the kind of deep struggle this monk-poet was having in attempting to grasp what it might mean for him to both reject ordinary society and, at the same time, remain attached to the prospects for social recognition of his obvious poetic skills. Additional affirmation of the latter had come in 1155, the year before "a great calamity shook society," when the poem he had written about "the guardhouse at famed Shirakawa gate," translated above, was selected for inclusion in a private *waka* collection, the *Goyōwaka-shū (Later Leaves of Waka Collection)*. This time the poem was clearly attributed to him.

During this period Saigyō, based at Mount Kōya but traveling freely as well, saw a need to comment not only on the larger trajectory of his times but also to offer advice to specific individuals. The dispatch of his own poems to persons he knew, even if by long distance, let him play the role of priest as well as friend. For instance, deaths in the Tokudaiji family to which he had early been so close, prompted him to write the following in 1161, advising Kin'yoshi to take the tonsure and become a monk. Saigyō himself was forty-four at the time.

During the period of mourning for his father, Tokudaiji Kin'yoshi's mother died as well. Having heard of this, I sent the following in condolence to him from Mount Kōya:

kasane kiru
fuji no koromo o
tayori nite
kokoro no iro o
someyo to zo omou   856

One on another
wisteria robes of mourning
ever deeper
suggest you might now dye
your life in the dharma's depth.

I received the following response from Tokudaiji Kin'yoshi

fujigoromo
kasanuru iro wa
fukakeredo
asaki kokoro no
shimanu hakanasa   857

The color of my
garments may have deepened,
but my mind
is still shallow, pale,
unfit for such a step.

If Saigyō interpreted a lull in the courtiers' poetic activities as a personal misfortune, there were other things consequent to the Hōgen Disturbance that he surely would have viewed as the onset of some kind of cultural and societal nightfall. For instance, almost immediately after their attempted coup, at least seventeen of Sutoku's supporters were killed in cold blood. This effectively put an end to what for three and a half centuries had been a ban on any capital punishment in the capital. And, as if to underscore the irony, policies such as the restoration of this punishment were pushed hardest by a man, Fujiwara Michinori (1106–60), who held office as Counselor of State even though he had been tonsured as a monk with the Buddhist name Shinzei. Kubota notes:

> To the courtiers in the capital, due to things like the outbreak of violence and the use of capital punishment on a large scale as advocated by Shinzei, it certainly seemed that a totally new epoch had been entered into. They noted as much in what they wrote in what were to become the historical records of the time.

Then, as if the point needed further emphasis, another bloody incident took place in the capital and surrounding areas in 1159, the Heiji Disturbance. It involved some of the warriors who were to figure largely in the pitched, protracted war between the Taira and Minamoto families during the 1180s. Although some institutional historians have recently suggested that the latter half of the twelfth century is too early a time to see epochal changes in Japanese society and have played down the impact of the Hōgen and Heiji Disturbances, within works written by persons living through those events, a *perception* of deep societal changes currently underway is clearly revealed.

Saigyō, perhaps more than any other, registered that perception in the poetry and prose he wrote between 1156 and his death in 1190. It is the verse of a man who, in spite of being a monk, remains keenly aware of what is happening within ordinary society and for the most part sees that society embarking on a downward slide. This too was probably linked to his conviction that things are not what they seem and that ironies abound. Being somewhat detached, both physically and socially, from the very center of things was not a bad way to see them more clearly. This appears to be why he wrote a poem such as the following:

haruka naru
iwa no hazama ni
hitori ite
hitometsutsu made
mono omowabaya   2079 [1099]

Boulder-encircled
space, so far from everything
that here I'm all alone:
a place where none can view me
but I can review all things.

The impulse to put distance between himself and the capital resulted in another journey, this time westward and on to the island of Shikoku. At age fifty-one he departed with a sense that he might never return. It had been exactly twenty-eight years since his tonsure. Before leaving the capital he wrote:

Just as had always been so, I continued to go to the Kamo Shrine even after becoming a monk. Now at an advancing age, I was about to pilgrimage to Shikoku, thinking that I may never return. So I made a night visit to this shrine on the tenth day of the tenth month of 1168. I wanted to present a votive request. But since I was wearing the clothes of a Buddhist monk and could not go inside the shrine, I requested someone to present it on my behalf. Through the trees the light of the moon was filtering softly, so that the atmosphere of the place was even more sacred than usual, and I was deeply moved. I wrote this:

kashikomaru
shide ni namida no
kakaru kana
mata itsuka wa to
omou aware ni   1181

Awe is what fills me
as my tears fall onto the sacred

branch I here present:
my feelings are of someone
wondering if he'll ever return.

This journey was to result in very important poetry. Part of its purpose was to pay homage to two persons who, although now dead, had been important to Saigyō. The first was Retired Emperor Sutoku, who, after his exile to Sanuki Province on Shikoku in 1156, had died in 1164, four years prior to Saigyō's journey. Arriving at this place the former emperor had purportedly lived, Saigyō wrote:

Having come to Sanuki, I was at a place called the Cove of Matsuyama. I looked around for the exact location where the Retired Emperor had resided, but no trace of his earlier presence could be found.

matsuyama no
nami ni nagarete
koshi fune no
yagate munashiku
narinikeru kana   1444

The ship he was on
crossed the waves to Matsuyama
and then suddenly
disappeared—as he too slipped
down below our horizon.

The best-known of his verses written during this journey was recycled later into the *Hōgen Monogatari,* a war tale likely composed during the next century, and in *Matsuyama Tengu,* a Noh drama. It was:

I was performing a service at [Sutoku's] gravesite at Shiramine.

yoshiya kimi
mukashi no tama no
yuka totemo

kakaran nochi wa
nanika wa sen   1446

Let it be, my lord.
Surely this is nothing
like the jewel-floored
palaces of your past, but can
anything alter what's occurred?

Addressed to the deceased monarch, one can detect in this poem a desire to console and pacify his spirit. It seems there was already a growing concern that the resentful and restless spirit of Sutoku, who not only had been shamed by exile but also had died in a distant location without the requisite Buddhist funerary rites, might have been causing a spate of calamities in the capital. Cameron Hurst notes: "As in the case of all unsettled political situations in traditional Japan, the chronicles record an unusual number of natural calamities and portents for the period: fires, comets, pestilence, and the like. The physical violence that had come to characterize life in the capital continued unabated."

Concern about this became increasingly acute over the years, so much so that in 1171 an effort was made to appease Sutoku's aggrieved spirit through public remembrance of him, even on the part of his former foes. The Saigyō poem just quoted figures significantly into this. Accompanied by this monk's provision of proper rituals of condolence and consolation at the gravesite, the poem in effect counsels the raging royal spirit to become pacific and at rest. If it is correct that the date for this action is 1168, then it appears that Saigyō was doing this because there were already reports of Sutoku's anger causing troubles in the capital. Alternatively, his composition of this poem, especially after it became known to others, may, in fact, have been the origin of society's growing concern that something had to be done to honor and appease the exiled ruler. In either case, this verse has considerable historical importance.

The poems he wrote about Sutoku's exile and sorry fate are strongly worded. They hint at the unjust treatment befallen him, yet at the same time speculate whether one of whom he had felt so fond might nevertheless have committed serious moral misdeeds. Was his fate a karmic consequence of past behavior?

Though his poems offer no direct proof, Saigyō was decidedly not in thrall to notions of a charmed life enjoyed by members of the imperial court. Were these later verses the fruit of further reflection upon his days as Norikiyo? Even in poems exchanged with courtiers back in the capital or with former courtiers who themselves had now taken the tonsure, his tone, while not that of a jeremiad, is straightforward. "People-who-lived-above-clouds" was one of the usual euphemisms for members of the imperial court. But negative karma, Saigyō suggests, was accumulating. And there would be prices to pay.

Within a set of six poems, perhaps from this period, on the topic of the six tiers of existence within Buddhist cosmology, Saigyō wrote of the imperial courtiers as belonging within the category of "heavenly beings"—that is, above ordinary humans, bellicose titans, animals, hungry ghosts, and creatures in hell. Yet, contrary to most courtier poets' endless celebration of their own sensitivities as justifying the "good life" they led, Saigyō adheres to traditional Buddhist teaching on this matter. His poem warns that life for them in their heavenly palaces is ephemeral, and descent through the states of existence happens easily and quickly.

Concerning Heavenly Beings

> *kumo no ue no*
> *tanoshimi tote mo*
> *kahi zo naki*
> *sate shimo yagate*
> *sumishi hateneba*
> 984

> The above-the-clouds
> life is surely joy itself
> but tempered
> by knowing life even there
> cannot go on forever.

But our account needs to return to what transpired during his journey to Shikoku. The second person whose memory he wished to honor there was Kūkai, the early Japanese transmitter of esoteric or tantric Buddhism and the founder of Japan's Shingon School. The fact that Kūkai seems to have been the only early "founder" figure to whom Saigyō paid such deep respect suggests that, although fairly eclectic in his approach to Buddhist teachings and practices, he felt a special affinity for Kūkai, the monastery on Mount Kōya that he founded, and the Shingon School in general. In any case, there is a sharp contrast between the poet's sadness in remembering Sutoku and his encounter with places sacred to the memory of Kūkai. The latter are strikingly positive, even ecstatic. Take, for instance, the following, in which Saigyō refers to Kūkai with the honorific title "Kōbō Daishi" (Great Teacher Kōbō).

I was in the province of Sanuki and in the mountains where Kōbō Daishi had once lived. While there, I stayed in a hut I had woven together out of grasses. The moon was especially bright and, looking in the direction of the [Inland] Sea, my vision was unclouded.

kumori naki
yama nite umi no
tsuki mireba
shima zo kōri no
taema narikeru   1447

Cloudfree mountains
encircle the sea, which holds
the reflected moon:
this transforms islands into
emptiness holes in a sea of ice.

The fact that Saigyō was positioned high enough to look down on an array of smaller islands, themselves in a sea formed within two much larger islands, is the positional starting point for this extraordinary poem. But Saigyō does not so much record the natural beauty as turn what he sees into a transmogrified vision. The state of his mind appears to be ecstatic—perhaps because the nexus with Kūkai has begun to suggest to him that what lies before his eyes is not unlike a mandala brought into being by natural forms. The unparalleled brightness of the moon creates an unusual limpidity in the poet's mind, resulting in a mode of visual and mental play. Suddenly the waters of the sea seem transformed into a massive plane of ice, and the islands therein seem no longer convex but now concave. Their darkened presence within the space of the glistening span of the sea makes them appear as holes within a vast sheet of ice. And *taema,* the last line's word for "interstice" or "hole," is sufficiently resonant with the Buddhist notion of *sunyata* or "emptiness" that this word insinuates into the poem a motif of higher-level unity of things that had looked separate on lower levels. The poem is, in the best sense of that word, "metaphysical." But that it has a cerebral dimension does not mean it was not rooted in profound and ecstatic experience. The natural setting undergoes a kind of beatification here.

The link with Kūkai across a span of three centuries becomes even more intense. Saigyō writes:

The climb up to Mandala Temple in order to carry out the activities proper for a pilgrim there was an unusually difficult one. The climber must make what seems like an almost perpendicular ascent. On the peak are buried sacred sutras that Kōbō Daishi copied out with his own hand. Outside the priest's quarters [at the top] is a ten-foot-square dais. It is said that Kōbō Daishi climbed up on to this every day in order to perform austerities. In order for others to perform devotional activities on it [without risk of falling off], a double enclosure has been constructed. Nevertheless, the dangers one faces in making a climb up to this place are truly extraordinary. I, for one, made my way to the top by crawling along on all fours.

> *meguriawan*
> *koto no chigiri zo*
> *arigataki*
> *kibishiki yama no*
> *chikai miru ni mo* 1461

Amazing to have made it
here to this point where

holy ones convened;
pledges are best when made
on precipices above it all.

Saigyō writes of this place as the high point in a most literal way of his journey to Shikoku but also as the apex of what made it important to him spiritually. He is impressed by the extent of what were reputed to be Kūkai's daily meditations after climbing up a precarious route. But, since lore had it that on this very spot a buddha had once come via clouds to link up with the esoteric master, Saigyō writes a poem about preternatural meetings. The implied sense is that, if Kūkai on this above-it-all location could meet a buddha, then Saigyō himself could entertain the belief that he, on this same spot, was now in some way linking up with Kūkai. Probably in no other place in the writings of Saigyō do we find so strong an expression of belief in supernatural possibilities. Of course, by this time pious accounts of pilgrims on Shikoku fortuitously meeting the long-ago deceased master Kūkai on the road were common. After an ascent on a path that struck him as death-defying, Saigyō's sensibility flattens out the difference between himself as living and persons purportedly dead. And he makes note of his own good karma in having reached such a place.

Another monk, Saijū, had been a traveling companion of his for a good part of the Shikoku journey but soon after this seems to have returned to the capital. Saigyō went on, but in a more leisurely fashion. And as he did so, he observed ordinary life and reflected on what he saw. The lengthy prose headnotes not only contextualize the poems but also make his work resemble a travel diary. His powers of observation of the lives of commoners, hardly something to the taste of most courtiers, were becoming sharper. But because most of the common people with whom he had contact were fisherfolk, he expresses a consistent concern for them as people whose livelihood compelled them to take the lives of fish and shellfish for food. Because he uses the term for "sin" *(tsumi)* liberally in these poems, at first sight what he writes about these people of the sea can seem harsh, too easy a condemnation from someone in a priestly class. But the poems turn into expressions of far greater ambivalence—and thus of understanding—when it is realized that *tsumi* has another sense altogether in that it can refer to a "large catch" and, therefore, connote something of the joy a fisherman feels in making a substantial haul.

When I crossed to Kojima Island in Bizen Province, I found myself in a place where men earned their living by catching minuscule shrimp called *ami*. I witnessed each fisherman attaching a bag to a long pole and putting this into the water. They had a name for the first among them to pull this device out of the water; they called him "first pole." And the one privileged to lift up the initial pole was the most senior among them. This [life-taking] act was referred to by them as a "lifting up," and this struck me deeply [because we used the same word for the prayers and religious vows we "lift up"]. I was moved beyond my ability to express well in words but, with tears in my eyes, I wrote this poem:

tatesomuru
ami toru ura no
hatsusao wa
tsumi no naka ni mo
suguretaruran   1463

Now lifting out
of the bay a haul of shrimp
is the first man's pole:
it looks to be a huge catch—
but one of sins as well.

Kubota is dissatisfied with critics who have judged poems such as this "too conceptual"—especially if by that is meant a mere articulation of Buddhist teachings and ideas. He argues, instead, that Saigyō in such poems is creating an *interface between* such conceptualizations and the concrete reality of the life and livelihood of these people. He knows the traditional Buddhist teachings about such things but is also massively impressed, even emotionally moved, by the dedicated hard work of people who have no choice but to live through the taking of animal life. This would, I suggest, apply to the following verse as well.

I was at a place where, out on the open sea, divers were snatching abalone from rocks under the water.

iwa no ne ni
kataomomuki ni
namiukite
awabi o kazuku
ama no muragimi   1468

Hanging on for life
to the rocks under them,
abalone face
the master diver swimming
down to pry them loose.

Either through misinformation or merely as a literary device, Saigyō takes
the row of apertures on the top of an abalone's shell to be that creature's
eyes. He then makes use of this to give us a vivid portrait of humans and these
beings of the sea engaged in a life-and-death struggle. They face off against
one another under water. The term used to express the way these two are fac-
ing one another suggests a situation not unlike that of two heroic warriors
about to battle to the death—as, for instance, in the *Tales of the Heike.*

Physical strength and the single-minded determination of a hero are
depicted on both sides of this struggle, and the poet's admiration for these
qualities in both comes through. He is not so much abandoning the Buddhist
teaching about nonviolence as suggesting that at times it can run up against
another quality that humans hold as virtuous—namely physical courage and
a strong will. He has no easy answer.

But why does Saigyō turn to such a topic? I suggest that it is because it,
at least as refracted through his life, was the dilemma not only of fisherfolk
on a faraway island but increasingly that of his associates back in the cap-
ital. Questions of violence, the taking of life, and murder had become
acutely relevant and painful. The courtiers were increasingly living their
own lives within a warrior ethos—in part because warriors were in their
employ no longer just to guard the frontiers and the palaces but to carry
out specific acts of homicide within the capital itself. And monks from one
temple were confronting and killing those of other temples. During his
Shikoku journey Saigyō had worked to pacify Sutoku's spirit and had
strengthened his own deep devotion to Kūkai. But he had carried with

him his existential concern for what was happening to Japanese society more generally and for what might need to be done about the ever more obvious human proclivity for violence.

After his journey to Shikoku, Saigyō probably reestablished himself in a hermitage at Mount Kōya, although in 1171 he records a visit to Sumiyoshi Shrine. As will be discussed below, this was perhaps an early indication of what was to become for this Buddhist monk an increasingly important linkage between Buddhism and Shinto.

It seems likely that during the following year, 1172, Saigyō took part in a Buddhist ceremony, actually something of an extravaganza, connected to the opening of greater trade with China. Such was the pet project of Taira Kiyomori (1118–81), and Saigyō was present at a service involving a thousand monks at this man's invitation. And because Kiyomori so dominated the political scene in 1171 and was involved in things that would later effect Saigyō significantly, his career is worth a brief review.

Born the same year as Saigyō, Kiyomori was from a military family, but rumor had it that he, like Sutoku, was another product of Retired Emperor Shirakawa's multiple affairs. His Taira father, whether in fact or in name only, was handsomely rewarded in 1135 for having served the court by subduing pirates in western Japan, and Kiyomori too benefited from this. Among his own military accomplishments was being on the winning side in the Hōgen Disturbance of 1156, when he was allied with Shinzei and crushed the take-over attempt by Sutoku. In the subsequent Heiji Disturbance he was the leader of the victors, and soon his power was immense. He entered the courtly ranks and became Chancellor of the Realm in 1167. An illness and the prospect of death persuaded him the next year to become a lay monk in a ceremony at Mount Kōya, one that Saigyō may have witnessed. But he recovered and in no way relinquished any of his accumulated power. Kiyomori recognized the Inland Sea's potential for becoming a great protected site for the establishment of a flourishing trade with China, and he did much to develop the port known today as the city of Kobe, then known as [Ō]wada in the province of Tsu. Saigyō's record is as follows:

The lay monk Taira Kiyomori sponsored a Buddhist service in which a thousand monks with expertise in the recitation of the *[Lotus] Sutra* took part. It was in Wada in Tsu Province. This was followed by the ritual of lighting ten thousand lamps. With nightfall these would die out, but one by one they would all be lit once again.

kienubeki
nori no hikari no
tomoshibi o
kakaguru wada no
tomari narikeri   934

The way of lamps
is to flicker and die in time,
but these of the dharma
shed light again here at Wada,
anchorage in the night.

Although it involves our making a temporary jump over some extraordinarily important material, Saigyō's next overt reference to Kiyomori is in sharp contrast to the felicitous occasion of the poem above. In 1180 Kiyomori, at that point in an increasingly threatened military and political position, arbitrarily declared that the capital itself would no longer be in Heian but henceforth at Fukuhara, the location of his own Taira family headquarters, also close to today's Kobe. He dragged along not only the core of the state bureaucracy but even the child emperor, who was under something like house arrest. Naturally, persons who felt the capital should remain where it had been for nearly four hundred years were scarcely pleased. Saigyō worded his own displeasure in a poem.

When I heard while at Ise that the capital had been moved to Fukuhara, I wrote the following about the moon:

kumo no ue ya
furuki miyako to
narinikeri
sumuran tsuki no
kage wa kawarade   2124

"Above-the-Cloud-Ones"—
   a name for courtiers of a capital
   that is no longer,
   but still true of the brilliant moon,
   which, unchanging, remains in place.

By going back again a bit in time, we can explore what had transpired to bring about something as drastic as an attempt to move the capital. Near the end of 1179 Kiyomori, already powerful, engineered what was tantamount to a coup and dismissed many of the courtiers in state positions. He put Go-Shirakawa, the retired emperor at that time, under house arrest, and for much of the time he was required to remain under guard within the Taira family precincts. Kiyomori had his own grandson, only two years old at the time, put on the throne. These acts solidified those opposed to him. The warriors of the Minamoto clan, also known as the Genji, while once allied with the Taira, were now resolutely their enemies. Reports reached the capital of a huge build-up of Minamoto forces in Japan's eastern provinces. And during the fateful year of 1180, what were at first skirmishes escalated into a full-blown war between the Taira and the Minamoto, which did not end until the land was much bloodied and the Taira were forced into total defeat in 1185. This was the worst internal warfare Japan had ever witnessed, and some of its major episodes, by literary embellishment, became oral narratives and then a war epic, the *Tales of the Heike,* a Japanese classic.

Saigyō, much more ready than his fellow poets to relate his verse to contemporaneous events, puts the matter directly and simply:

In the world of men it came to be a time of warfare. Throughout the country—west, east, north, and south—there was no place where the war was not being fought. The count of those dying because of it climbed continually and reached an enormous number. It was beyond belief! And for what on earth was this struggle taking place? A most tragic state of affairs:

shide no yama
koyuru taema wa
araji kashi

nakunaru hito no
kazu tsuzukitsutsu 1868

There's no gap or break
in the ranks of those marching
under the hill:
an endless line of dying men,
coming on and on and on....

Moreover, his attention could be turned to specific stages of the war and scenes of battle—at least as these had been reported to him. An early battle in 1180 was fought near the famous bridge at Uji, south of the capital. It was technically won by the Taira, who took pride in it. Although he probably fuses material from a number of skirmishes into his account—for instance a technique of using horses as substitute for a bridge—the crucial thing is that Saigyō was unimpressed with the ability of either side to really "win" in such contexts. His opposition to the utter insanity of such warfare was itself mounting. The headnote of his poem, critics agree, is sarcastic.

Warriors were marching off in great numbers into the mountain of death. Maybe so many will end up there that the mountain bandits will not dare show themselves [out of fear]. Ordinary people, then, can be unafraid. Maybe in this kind of world, things can *truly* be relied upon!

shizumu naru
shide no yama ga wa
minagirite
mumaigata mo ya
kanawazaruramu 1869

The river of death
is swollen with bodies
fallen into it;
in the end the bridge
of horses cannot help.

The sarcasm is thick. Knowing what he did about the history of warriors, he could recognize the irony in how the military, thought at one time to be protectors of the court and the general populace, had become so ambitious and contentious that the very people who relied on them for safety were now terrorized by their activities. Emperors they once defended they now hauled around in a state of house arrest. And the warrior Kiyomori arbitrarily relocated the capital itself.

Although it is beyond my purpose to detail the course of the war between the Taira and the Minamoto and bring to the fore the large cast of persons involved, there can be no doubt that it brought bloodshed and havoc to Japan on a scale not seen before. Numbers escalated. Minamoto Yoritomo, who eventually won out in the protracted struggle, had a force of two hundred thousand men at one point. And even though there was a lull in the fighting between its outbreak in 1180 and renewed ferocity in 1183, the society as a whole was in a continuous state of upheaval. Eventually, among a concentration of forces in the Inland Sea in a showdown between ship-based warriors, a decisive battle was fought. On the twenty-third day of the third lunar month in 1185 at a place called Dannoura at the far western end of that sea, the Taira forces were battled down. They were literally driven into the sea and took along with them Emperor Antoku, aged eight at the time, and—so it is said—some of the royal regalia. All disappeared into the waters.

In contrast to the *Tales of the Heike,* which would locate high drama in this and find elements of beauty in the battles—even going so far as to compare the colored silks in the battle garb of drowned samurai to the "brocade" of maple leaves dancing on surging waters—Saigyō was nothing if not utterly realistic about war. Knowing as he did the life of the warrior, one he had intentionally left, it struck him as naïve for others to have placed themselves and their civilized society under the "protection" of samurai types.

It was likely during this same period that he composed a set of poems under the rubric "Seeing the Pictures in a Hell-Screen," and these poems bolster such conclusions. For these verses are not only replete with references to the implements of war but also show the poet in a mood of sustained reflection upon the karmic effect of having had his own origins in a family of samurai. The poems, in essence, forge a union: Hell is war and, conversely, war is hell. These poems, employing diction about as alien as possible from the norm in "court poetry," form a striking, even gripping, sequence. Here

I select from it two highly personalized ones. Both are prefaced by prose headnotes saying they were inspired when the poet saw the various hells depicted in a painting.

> *tarachio no*
> *yukue o ware mo*
> *shiranu kana*
> *onaji honoo ni*
> *museburamedomo*
>
> 1855

> I wish I knew
> the fate of my father,
> and I'd like
> to know too if his place
> in flames will also be mine.

There seems to be something more here than the quasi-formalized sentiments of a dutiful son. Saigyō, who can be assumed to have performed rites to pacify his deceased warrior father, Noriyasu, seems to be existentially worried that the warrior, in a killing profession by definition, may have a karmic burden so great that it cannot be easily removed. And that, in turn, makes him anxious about his own future. This degree of personalized concern carries over, I suggest, in how we should understand the next poem as well.

> *konomi mishi*
> *tsurugi no eda ni*
> *nobore tote*
> *shimoto no hishi o*
> *mi ni tatsuru kana*
>
> 1845

> Swords on which my eyes
> once fastened with delight are
> here branches of trees
> ascended by bodies being flogged
> by barb-studded whips.

Here the poet assumes a readership already familiar with a genre of painting that depicted one kind of future punishment as the extension and intensification of what in this present life comes as the pain of unfulfilled desire. The specific kind of picture, of which extant copies remain, showed a tree with men climbing up and down it. Their motivation for doing so was women, either gorgeously or scantily clad, who would appear first at the top of such trees and then, once the men had drawn close, would suddenly disappear only to be found now at the bottom. The Buddhist equivalent of Tantalus here had taken on an eroticized form. But what made this especially hellish for these eternally frustrated men was the fact that the branches of the depicted tree were, in fact, swords. And these would repeatedly lacerate the flesh of these men pressing their own bodies against them in their mad ascent and descent in lustful pursuit. Demons on the scene would add to the excruciating pain by prodding and whipping these men into accelerated movement.

Although Saigyō clearly refers to such a picture, he dramatically changes its signification. The grammar of the poem has the speaker making no reference to the attractiveness and allure of women but instead, surprisingly, to that of the sword. Reference to eros between the sexes is replaced with hints about the quasi-erotic feelings a warrior might have for his own sword or for swords in general. And the sentiments of the speaker in this poem—presumably Saigyō himself—are that such allure is now in the past. He once took delight in these swords, but that is no longer the case.

When we recall what we know about the transformation of Norikiyo into Saigyō, the poem provides insight. On the first level it is an implicit recapitulation of his personal decision to replace the warrior life with that of a Buddhist monk committed to nonviolence. But, in addition, the style of this poem forces acknowledgment that the professional warrior ethos ineluctably signifies desire, capitulation to desire, and horrible human suffering. Saigyō appears to have recognized that to become inured to the "glories" of the military life occurs through enculturation and through the indoctrination of very young minds. Quoted at the outset of this account but worth repeating here is a poem Saigyō probably wrote during the years when warfare convulsed the land:

Toy bamboo bow
in hand, a mere child takes

aim at a sparrow
and already longs to wear
a warrior's headgear.

This fits in well, I suggest, with what he was now writing about "swords on which my eyes / once fastened with delight."

We today know a fair amount about the way in which, especially during the centuries subsequent to Saigyō's death, Japanese Buddhists accommodated their Buddhism to the ethos of the warrior. Certain figures in the Zen tradition in particular appear to have waived what should have been a concern about bloodshed and found reasons to prize and praise the way of the warrior. Takuan Sōhō (1573–1645) sometimes wrote about the mind and the sword in a way that, at least to some critics, sanctions the samurai who would make the latter into something of a fetish. And otherwise honorable figures such as Hakuin (1686–1769) opened their writings to skepticism from war-wary critics in our own day when they celebrated the samurai even as a model to be emulated by the monk.

I suggest that Saigyō lived at a point when such an affirmation of the warrior had begun, and offer the poem below as evidence. But, if so, it is also clear that he himself emphatically rejected such a trend. Again we have a poem that in all likelihood derives from the period, between 1180 and 1185, when warfare between the Taira and the Minamoto was foisting great suffering upon many. At this time Saigyō, often in an exchange of verse with distant correspondents, was composing linked verses. In this instance he provides concluding lines to the first section of a poem that had been sent to him for that purpose. The headnote gives us the context, itself important.

The young courtiers associated with retired princess Jōsaimon-in had been discussing with her palace guard the impact the wars' tumult was having on the writing of verse. So when the moon was especially brilliant, efforts were made to write *renga* [linked verses] precisely about such war-making. This initial portion of linked verse arose from this process:

ikusa o terasu
yumihari no tsuki   1871

Shaped like a crossbow pulled tight
the moon lights up a battle below...

Someone came to visit me while I was in Ise and said: "The foregoing lines of linked verse are being recited by the palace guard, but no one has been able to complete it successfully." Hearing this, I wrote the following [complementary] lines:

kokorokiru
te naru kohori no
kage nomi ka   1871 *continued*

Does real light come
via an icy, hand-held blade
or from another source?

Sarcasm regarding human folly is here, too, not far from the surface. Saigyō picks up on the submitted lines' theme of "night" as the context for a battle between warriors. He then drives home a sharp contrast between the sheer folly of being fascinated by heavy metal—however much it may gleam and glisten in that night—and the higher, far more comprehensive kind of enlightenment that might come to humans ready to emulate the illumination, always a pacific one, provided by the moon. Kubota Shōichirō writes of there being in this poem "an intense rejection of the sheer foolishness represented by war, itself something that should be viewed as nothing other than an ugly concentration of all of mankind's illusions."

In two of the poems translated just above, Saigyō makes reference to being at Ise, not Mount Kōya, when writing a poem for someone in the capital. He moved in 1180 when he was sixty-three years old. He tells us something about it in a poem, one that Fujiwara Shunzei (1114–1204), surely the doyen of court poets at that time, included in his own personal anthology, the *Senzaiwaka-shū,* a work begun in the early 1170s, held up by the Taira-Minamoto wars, and then finally presented to the throne in 1187. Saigyō had written:

I grew tired of living on Mount Kōya and went to a mountain temple at a place called Futami in the vicinity of Ise. The sacred mountain of the great Shinto shrine there is referred to as the mountain traversed by sacred beings. Reflecting on the fact that the great goddess Amaterasu, who is worshiped at the imperial shrine in Ise, is a manifest expression of Dainichi Buddha, I composed the following:

fukaku irite
kamiji no oku o
tazunureba
mata ue mo naki
mine no matsukaze   2108

Following the paths
the gods passed over, I seek
their innermost place;
up and up to the highest of all:
peak where wind soughs through pines.

Clearly an important question is why Saigyō, a Buddhist monk linked—intellectually and emotionally—to Mount Kōya and its founder, Kūkai, would abruptly change the venue of his life and composition to an area connected to Ise, the most important Shinto shrine. The question becomes even more pointed when it is recalled that Buddhist priests, if in religious garb, were not permitted to enter the sacred shrines of Shinto. Saigyō himself, as noted above, met with this prohibition when he wanted to present a prayer to the gods at the Kamo Shrine in the capital.

Earlier scholars pursuing the reasons for the poet-monk's move suggested that internal rivalries among high ranking monks at Mount Kōya as well as strife between Kōya and other religious institutions had become pronounced. And to Saigyō, given what we know about him, this was deeply distasteful. Although Kubota Jun finds problems in such hypotheses because the recorded outbreak of most such strife actually postdated Saigyō's move to Ise, it nonetheless seems probable that an atmosphere of rivalry had become increasingly intense at Kōya, and his response was to leave. In addition, two monk-poets who had been his closest friends there had died by 1180. Saigyō's reasons for remaining had surely thinned.

Not only did conditions at Kōya encourage Saigyō to leave, but there were also reasons why Saigyō was drawn *to* Ise. One of these was surely his close and probably longstanding relationship with members of the Arakida family, which had served as hereditary priests of the inner Ise Shrine from as early as the eighth century. Theoretically a Buddhist priest was supposed to remain outside the Ise Shrine, but this seems not to have inhibited the forming of such a relationship. In fact, members of the Arakida family themselves appear to have had a strong interest in Buddhism. And Arakida Mitsuyoshi, the one with closest ties to Saigyō, himself was tonsured as a monk named Ren'a later in life.

During his time at Ise, Saigyō mentored members of the Arakida family and was the direct tutor of Mitsuyoshi in the practice of poetry. This was appropriate for, by this point in his life, Saigyō's skills as one of the era's finest poets were at last being recognized publicly. His own inclusion in the era's verse collections no doubt facilitated acceptance of poems by his pupil, Mitsuyoshi. This professional and occupational dimension of his move to Ise and seven-year residence there is signifcant.

There was also, however, an intellectual reason. Japanese scholars looking into this question have emphasized what Saigyō himself said in the introduction and lines of the poem cited just above. These clearly put into poetry one of the central teachings of his time—namely, that the deities *(kami)* of Shinto are, when properly understood, manifestations of buddhas and bodhisattvas. The elaboration of this theory, beginning at least as early as the tenth century, had eased the way for many Japanese people to see no conceptual or cultic contradiction in identifying both with Buddhist temples and Shinto shrines. It is important that, although widely shared, this viewpoint was especially articulated in the esoteric Buddhism associated with Kūkai and Mount Kōya. Allan Grapard rightly points out that the energies invested in detailing the structure and workings of these relationships show the basic misconception of earlier writers in the West who took the whole as an incoherent "mishmash."

In Saigyō's work such specified doctrine and the poetic imagination come together. We can trace this in what he does within particular poems. The technical term for the concept of *kami* as manifestations of buddhas and bodhisattvas was *honji-suijaku; sui* fundamentally signifies a condition of "hanging down," or being "pendent." Relying upon our ability to recognize that whatever is pendent can only be so because it has something else as its "base" or "starting point," the theoreticians of Japan stressed that the *kami* associated with Shinto are the pendent phenomena *(suijaku)* but their base *(honji)* lies, in fact, in the enlightened beings treasured within the Indian Buddhist tradition. Thus, for instance, when a person worships Amaterasu, the sun goddess in the Shinto pantheon, he or she is simultaneously paying respect to Dainichi Nyorai (Mahavairochana Tathagata), the buddha who was held to have expounded the truth of esoteric Buddhism.

Saigyō rather brilliantly turns doctrine into a concretized image in his verse. He does so by noting how the branches or, perhaps, even the dangling stalks of early summer flowers of the *sakaki* tree, the variety of tree most sacred in Shinto, are literally pendent. They hang down from a base at the top of the tree. We perhaps can catch something of the union of concept and image if we note how our own language links being pendent with being interdependent. Saigyō wrote:

Having gone to Ise, I worshipped at the great shrine.

> *sakakiba ni*
> *kokoro o kakemu*
> *yūshidete*
> *omoeba kami mo*
> *hotoke narikeri*   1312

> Adoration for
> the sacred sakaki tree—
> pendant branches
> with both gods and buddhas
> depending on each other.

In some sense such poetry, by way of its presentation of a concrete image to the mind's eye, itself makes the "hard" concepts of religious or philo-sophical doctrine somehow "soft" and manifest. And, although a topic too vast to be entered into here, the capacity of a single poem to accomplish such deeds fits exactly into something else apparently real and meaningful to Saigyō—namely, the idea that *waka* poems were themselves a form of Buddhist *mantra*.

Ironically, although competition, even conflict, was becoming pronounced during the last decades of Saigyō's life on the *institutional* level, the official *doctrine* of the day insisted upon a fundamental unity on the deepest level between beings revered in the temples and the *kami* worshiped in shrines. And in that sense the ease of Saigyō's move from Kōya to Ise was both a personalized implementation of this irenic doctrine and, at the same time, a move to put behind himself an institution that seemed to be subverting that very teaching. And Saigyō, deeply disturbed by the growing strife in secular society, would naturally have been disappointed in religious contexts that followed suit and, conversely, drawn to one—in this case the Ise Shrine—that appeared to hold to the pluralistic, bridge-building agenda so important to him. The imagery of the following poem shows Saigyō's belief in Ise's capacity for both strength and clarity.

> *miyabashira*
> *shitatsu iwane ni*
> *shikitatete*
> *tsuyu mo kumoranu*
> *hi no mikage kana*   1903 [1877]

> Shrine pillar
> rooted firmly in the rocks;
> sun in the sky
> casting down a shaft of light
> never overcome by clouds.

It is, one may hope, not an intrusive interpretation to see in such a verse an implicit contrast between what the poet saw as Ise's peaceful ambience and the strife, both secular and religious, in most places elsewhere in his day.

Saigyō's embrace of the *honji-suijaku* teaching likely had a direct and personal consequence for how he came to view what had been a longstanding, irrepressible fondness for cherry blossoms, especially as these could be found along the valleys of Mount Yoshino, located on the same peninsula as both Mount Kōya and the Ise Shrine. Poems composed about the astonishing beauty of the blossoms observed there are abundant in Saigyō's work. And from time to time he expressed worries, either real or hypothetical, that his passion for these was tantamount to a deep-seated attachment, one that might be itself an obstacle to his spiritual disciplines and the realization of his goals as a Buddhist. An example of his expression of such a concern is the following:

While undertaking religious disciplines, I was in a place that had attractive blossoms:

> *nagamuru ni*
> *hana no nadate no*
> *mi narazuba*
> *kono moto nite ya*
> *haru o kurasan* 108

> If my rapt gaze
> would not give rise to rumor
> and disgrace, I'd
> want to spend all spring fixed here,
> feasting my eyes on these flowers.

It is, I think, not wrong to view Saigyō's efforts to make sense of his passion for the beautiful phenomena of the natural world, no doubt epitomized for him by the blossoms at Yoshino, as one of the major intellectual and religious concerns of his life. It was especially so because, in contrast to the intensifying strife and incivility that was enveloping "civil" society, the locations where he placed his hermitages and carried out his religious praxis seemed, by contrast, places of both peace and inherent beauty. He, I think, employed multiple strategies from within the Buddhist tradition in order to affirm the basic goodness and value of the natural world. And among these was the *honji-suijaku* concept. The logic appears to have been as follows: Since the Shinto *kami* are indeed manifestations of buddhahood and, since such *kami* are somehow present within all natural phenomena that impress us humans with their beauty and sacredness, then there need be no contradiction between even our most intense feelings for such things and efforts to move along the Buddhist path. Natural beauty is itself an articulation of the enlightened state. And to fall under its supposed "sway" is to be, when rightly understood, engaged in the practice of the true path.

Such reasoning, which engages the emotions as well as the mind, collapsed all distance—geographical, temporal, and spiritual—between the enlightenment of Shakyamuni in India centuries earlier and Saigyō's experinece on Yoshino, the site to which he was most "attached." Thus, in a verse that appears to have been composed after his move to Ise, he could write:

> *hana no iro no*
> *yuki-no-miyama ni*
> *kayoeba ya*
> *fukaki yoshino no*
> *oku e iraruru*   1706

> Do the white blossoms
> on my mountain take the place of
> snow on the holy Himalayas?
> I wish to enter the profound
> inner depths of Mount Yoshino.

We today may find puzzling an image of Shakyamuni positioned so high in the Himalayas that he was ensconced in snow. However, Saigyō, either because he was misinformed about where Shakyamuni had lived or because he simply liked the image, chose to fuse the whiteness of Yoshino's blossoms with the snow on Asia's highest peaks.

In 1186 Saigyō, now sixty-nine years old, undertook his last major journey, and it was once again to the far northeast, the area to which he had gone more than four decades earlier. Although he was now writing some of the best poetry of his entire career, the probable reason for undertaking such a strenuous journey at such an advanced age had less to do with giving him venues for writing and more to do with carrying out obligations as a monk. There is now general agreement that his travels involved the collection of funds from donors for the rebuilding of Tōdai-ji, perhaps Japan's grandest temple, built initially in Nara in 741.

But why was Tōdai-ji in need of rebuilding?

The reason for this too reflects the nature of the times. The fact is that it had been recently burned down. By the latter half of 1180, some major temples around the capital had become strongly opposed to the highhanded actions of the Taira. Monks were themselves rebellious and on the move. In response the Taira burned down or severely damaged the temples that housed these monks. Shigehira (1156–85), one of the sons of Taira Kiyomori, led the attack. Mikael Adolphson writes:

> Although some courtiers were still apprehensive about sending troops to Nara and were clearly hoping for, perhaps even expecting, a peaceful solution because of the apparent superiority of the Taira forces, Shigehira was now determined to deal the rebellious temples a crippling blow. On the twenty-seventh day of the twelfth month of 1180, he attacked Tōdaiji before turning his attention to Kōfukuji at the end of the day. Both temples were heavily damaged, as several buildings were burned to the ground....

Within a single day two of Japan's most impressive architectural achievements had been substantially destroyed. News of the magnitude of this event shook the land, and people, already viewing events with alarm, found proof herein that the "age of the final [weakened] Dharma" *(mappō)* had been entered. Paul Varley writes: "To people living in the age of *mappō* and the Gempei War, the burning of these temples—one patronized by the imperial family, the other by the Fujiwara—appeared to symbolize the destruction of Japanese civilization itself."

Finally by 1185 the wars had ended. And already during the following year Saigyō, now with a considerable reputation both as a poet and a man of religion, appears to have participated in efforts at rebuilding. One reason that he solicited contributions in the northeast was the continued presence in that area of members of his own larger family, some of whom were wealthy.

Fortunately his travels also resulted in some superb poetry, many items of which came to the attention of the persons in court who would soon thereafter be putting together the *Shinkokin-shū,* ordered in 1201 and surely one of the best imperial collections of verse. As an indication of the regard given him, Saigyō is represented in it by ninety-four poems—an allocation greater than any other poet within it. One poem of that period is the following:

While on the way to the far north to visit people I knew there, I was at Saya-no-naka yama [Mount Dead-o'-Night] and I remembered the past:

> *toshi takete*
> *mata koyubeshi to*
> *omoiki ya*
> *inochi narikeri*
> *saya-no-naka yama*   2130 [987]

> Little did I guess
> I'd ever pass so many years...
> or even this mountain
> again, in one, now long, life:
> here on Mount Dead-o'-Night.

Saigyō's description of himself traversing this road as an old man gives an added level of gravity to his being in a place already well known for necessitating a treacherous valley descent and ascent. Its narrow, rugged path was often described as "death-defying." Saigyō's contemporaries were aware of the reputation of Saya-no-naka yama, in what is now Shizuoka. One source of their knowledge would have been a poem by Ki no Tomonori (fl. ca. 890) included in the great *Kokin-shū* imperial anthology. The relevant poem has been translated by Laurel Rasplica Rodd as follows:

why have I begun
to love so recklessly　like
　one lost in the night
Middle Mountain of the Night
on the road to Azuma

Being also frequented by bandits, this location offered multiple risks—
and to be traversing it in the dead of night was, for a man so advanced in
years, no small challenge. The reason this poem was so striking to Saigyō's
contemporaries lay, however, in the level of equanimity expressed. The man
going into this dangerous valley was also, by an obvious analogy, facing
death, even if only a natural one, in the near future. What in the *Kokin-shū*
poems stands forth as the "recklessness" of love, which is compared to going
through a dangerous place *imagined* by the poet, has in Saigyō's poem
become a kind of spiritual bravery that gives him a readiness to make his
descent into the actual location of real, palpable hazards. And the "night" into
which he steps so resolutely is, given all this, also the poet's death, certainly
not far in his future.

Fond at this point of making both parallels and contrasts with earlier
phases of his life, Saigyō now composed a poem that seems to locate an ele-
ment of humor, not bitter irony, in his own present condition.

takeuma o
tsue ni mo kyō wa
tanomu kana
warawa asobi o
omoiidetsutsu   1810

Propped up by my cane,
I hobble along remembering
my boyhood when
I loved playing horseman
on a piece of long bamboo.

A nearly contemporaneous drawing provides us with a good sense of
just how children of that era played "horse." This verse, like the probably

contemporaneous one beginning "Toy bamboo in hand," shows us a poet whose conscious acts of recollection, reaching back to his own childhood, are in a real way attempts to put together the contour of a whole life. And these efforts, fortunately not just kept to himself but inscribed into poems for us to read, show us a person more and more at ease with the fact that his own life may be swiftly coming to its end.

This motif is exquisitely present in a verse that Saigyō appears to have regarded as his favorite among his works. He wrote:

While undertaking religious exercises in the eastern region, I wrote the following in view of Mount Fuji:

> *kaze ni nabiku*
> *fuji no keburi no*
> *sora ni kiete*
> *yukue mo shiranu*
> *waga omoi kana*   2138 [1613]

> The wisps of smoke from Fuji
> yield to the wind and lose themselves
> in sky, in emptiness,
> which takes as well the aimless passions
> that through my life burned deep inside.

This verse does extraordinary things within its small scope. Writing at a time when Fuji, not then in its current dormancy, was showing its volcanic nature by means of a thin column of smoke arising from its crater, Saigyō takes advantage of what is known about the hot core of such mountains. That is, he draws a parallel between Fuji and himself—since, in the last line of the original, the term *omoi* denotes both thoughts and emotions. And, thus, since this is a poem of personalized retrospection, Saigyō refers to the passions that had been so much a part of his own life. (This sense is reinforced by the fact that the term here transliterated as *omoi* was then pronounced as *omohi* and, as such, had present within it the sound *hi*, meaning "fire.")

Astutely the poet suggests that, parallel to the fire in the mountain before which he sits or stands, there had long been a different kind of "fire" within himself. The many poems by him referring to erotic encounters were not likely based on purely imagined events. In addition to interpersonal eros, Saigyō, as already noted, wrote often of the blossoms at Yoshino as having themselves stirred within him a monumental and inextinguishable passion. The *sakura* in full bloom had not only represented quintessential beauty but could also arouse something flamelike within him.

Yet the poem, having created this striking image, moves on to suggest that in some ways the poet has moved now to a different phase of life. He is ready to relinquish things. Just as the smoke from the volcano is portrayed as wafting into the sky and disappearing there, so too the poet puts himself in the mental frame of someone at ease with his own departure from this life. And since *sora,* the word for "sky," is written with a Chinese character signifying as well what Buddhists have meant when talking positively about *sunyata,* or "emptiness," this religious signification is subtly present in the diction of the verse. The passion arises but is then encompassed within an ambit of peace and tranquillity.

When Saigyō traveled on he appears to have stopped in Kamakura, and it is in that connection that there survives what purports to be an accurate and detailed historical record of something unusually interesting that transpired there. It is an account of a meeting between this traveling monk and Minamoto Yoritomo (1147–99), the warrior primarily responsible for the defeat of the Taira in 1185 and now, one year later, rapidly become the strong man who would have *de facto* hegemony over a great deal of Japan. Later in 1192 he would be designated by the emperor as the "barbarian-subduing general," a term that in shortened form we know as *shōgun.* Once institutionalized, the shogunate would come to dominate the whole of Japan's political and social life through the medieval and early modern periods. It would not end until 1867.

Yoritomo was the first in this line. After the collapse of his enemies, the Taira, he kept his administrative headquarters in the town of Kamakura, actually little more than a military encampment at that time. In fact, he appears to have been satisfied with power and not very interested in gaining the kinds of titles that earlier warriors had so much coveted.

In any case he was in Kamakura in 1186 when Saigyō passed through on his way north. What follows is a translation of their meeting according to the *Azuma Kagami (Mirror of Eastern Japan)*, a chronicle of the Kamakura shogunate composed during the thirteenth century but covering the years between 1180 and 1266. Often reliable but with obvious lacunae and semi-fictive sections, we today can neither confirm nor disconfirm the truth of what follows:

> The fifteenth day of the eighth month of the second year of the Bunji era [1186], sixth calendrical sign, second zodiac sign. When Minamoto Yoritomo went to pay homage at the shrine of Tsurugaoka [in Kamakura], there was an elderly monk who was wandering around there in the vicinity of the shrine's *torii* gate. Yoritomo was curious about this and, because of the demeanor of the monk, had Kagesue make an inquiry to find out the man's name. He learned that the monk was Officer-of-the-Guard Satō Norikiyo, now a priest named Saigyō. Yoritomo, therefore, sent a message informing this man that he was to be granted an amicable audience with himself and telling him, moreover, that during their upcoming meeting Saigyō was expected to discourse about poetry. Saigyō then let Yoritomo know that he accepted this invitation. Then he continued visiting shrines and temples, performing acts of religious devotion. Because he had issued this invitation to this man, Yoritomo and his party immediately returned to his mansion. Then on the occasion of the formal session at the mansion to which he had been invited, Saigyō was requested to discuss not only "the way of poetry" but also the arts of archery and horsemanship. Saigyō said the following:
>
>> As for skills with the bow and horses, at the beginning—that is, when I still led a secular life—I myself rather imperfectly practiced them and in this way carried on my family's tradition. However, I became disenchanted with secular life during the eighth month of the third year of the Hōen era [1137]; when that happened, those military skills handed down to me—inasmuch as I was the ninth-generation direct heir of Ason Hidesato—were totally destroyed and lost forever. As the result of the karma of evil actions of the past, today not even

the slightest remnant of such things remains in the depths of my soul; they have all passed into complete oblivion. As for the writing of verses, it is nothing more than the composition of a mere thirty-one syllables when one is emotionally stirred by the sight of blossoms or the moon; I know nothing about "depths" in the composition of poetry. This being the case, it would be out of place for me to want to say more.

Nevertheless, Saigyō did not hesitate to show his gratitude for the favor that Yoritomo had extended to him, and he did, in fact, speak at length and in detail about archery and equestrian skills. Toshikane took down a record of the things that were said. The discussion of these matters lasted throughout the night.

The sixteenth day of the eighth month of the second year of the Bunji era, seventh calendrical sign, third zodiac sign; noon. Monk Saigyō took his leave. He was repeatedly asked to stay longer but would not. Yoritomo gave him a gift, a cat made out of silver. Saigyō gratefully accepted this gift, but when he was out beyond the gate, he gave the silver cat to a child who happened to be playing there. Having accepted an assignment from the Venerable Chōgen to solicit donations of gold dust for the rebuilding of Tōdai-ji Temple, Saigyō was headed north for Mutsu. He had made a pilgrim's stop at the Tsurugaoka shrine as this was on the best road for him to take north. Hidehira, the pious layman who was the governor of Mutsu, was a kinsman of Saigyō.

Mention of Hidehira at the end of this probably suggests Saigyō was keeping Yoritomo informed about his specific plans. It was a time when military alliances in the northeast were not yet completely settled, and Yoritomo, notoriously suspicious, may have thought Saigyō to be a traveling spy. Whether the monk received more than a silver cat from Yoritomo is less clear. Moreover, since precisely at the time of Saigyō's stopover Yoritomo was hosting *yabusame* as a kind of military sport in Kamakura, it may be that, because this was something in which the monk had been skilled in his youth, Yoritomo was checking on what the old monk still might know about high-speed equestrian archery. And since the *Azuma kagami* was written at a time when Saigyō was remembered as someone both saintly and courageous, the image therein of him being treated well by Yoritomo no doubt benefited the reputation of the shogun as well.

After his journey north Saigyō, with an enhanced reputation, met with important and interesting people. The *Seiashō,* a work of the fourteenth century, describes a meeting between Saigyō and the monk Mongaku, a fierce-tempered man who had accidentally killed a court lady and was subsequently known for tough training as a monk. He is said to have told his own monk trainees that he personally despised monks such as Saigyō who would write poetry. Mongaku boasted of being ready to bash in the poet's head if they ever met. In fact, Saigyō subsequently did attend a Buddhist service at Mongaku's temple, and the latter's trainees were quite surprised to see the two senior monks engaged in friendly conversation. Later, in questioning their master, they found he had nothing but praise for Saigyō.

That there may be authenticity in this story is suggested by documents showing that Saigyō did in fact spend time at Mongaku's temple, Jingō-ji in Takao. While there a record was made of his discussions with Myōe (1173–1232), a younger monk who studied under Mongaku and was destined to become one of the most important Buddhist thinkers of the medieval period. Saigyō, it seems, was being drawn into a variety of discussions about the role of poetry within the practice of Buddhism, a role he never seems to have tired of defending.

Because it has a bearing on what significance we may derive from the manner of Saigyō's death, a brief look at some distinctive aspects of his vision of humanity and the natural world seems relevant. First, I find great value in something noticed by Kubota Jun. He selects a group of poems that all have their setting fixed by the word *yamagatsu,* referring to poor and humble mountain folk. Kubota compares Saigyō's to poems such as the following from the *Kokin-shū.* The poem's author is unknown.

> *ana koishi*
> *ima mo miteshi ga*
> *yamagatsu no*

kakiho ni sakeru
yamato nadeshiko

Translated by Laurel Rasplica Rodd this poem becomes:

> oh sweet yearning if
> only I could meet here once
>   more…that delicate
> Japanese carnation that bloomed
> on the mountain peasant's fence

Kubota remarks that in such poems, typical of the court, the speaker places himself physically close to the fence or home of the *yamagatsu* peasant but, entirely caught up in his own affairs, pays absolutely no attention to the life of actual peasants. By contrast Saigyō writes of the *yamagatsu* in the following way:

> *yamagatsu no*
> *suminu to miyuru*
> *watari kana*
> *fuyu ni aseyuku*
> *shizuhara no sato*   1639

> What I see when I
> look around are the dwellings
> of poor mountain people:
> colors get faint in so quiet
> a village in mid-winter.

"Even when physically at a distance from them, Saigyō notices the people and their livelihood," writes Kubota. "There is in him an interest in their lives and a strong sense of compassion for them." It reminds us of the attention he paid to the lives of fisherfolk in Shikoku.

We can go farther. In a poem such as the one above, Saigyō does not see winter's removal of the rich colors of prior seasons as necessarily a loss, or as a diminution of beauty. Earl Miner rightly notes of this poet that he retains "a sense that even poor, frost-wasted reeds have a precious beauty" and that, more globally, "Saigyō is important (apart from the intrinsic appeal of his poems) in that he forecasts some of the main aesthetic preferences in later poetic form, especially in *haikai* and *haiku*." (This capacity to see the beauty in what is plain and almost void of color would in the later medieval period inform the *wabi* aesthetic of *cha-no-yu,* the Japanese practice that turns the serving and drinking of tea into acts of beauty.)

But why does Saigyō move things in this direction?

I suggest it has something to do with relinquishing—perhaps through Buddhist practices—the framework within which one set of things is viewed as desirable and their opposite as distasteful and to be avoided. In Saigyō even the sensibility shaping verse has been weaned away from the value-stacked polarities of ordinary society. Saigyō's sensitivity to the irony in human affairs is related to his awareness of what goes off track when we dichotomize reality. He was forced to see that even his own attempts to "leave the world" were, if naïvely misconstrued, attempts to find private peace in another such dichotomy. To transcend that habit of mind became the project of both his Buddhist practice and his writing of poetry during the later decades of his life. The "world" he had left behind was the world that bifurcated all things into what one subjectively liked or wanted on the one hand and what one disliked and disowned on the other. Therefore, even solitude had become tolerable and in its own way an aspect of reality to be cherished. This insight seems to lie behind the following poem:

> *furu hata no*
> *soba no tatsu ki ni*
> *iru hato no*
> *tomo yobu koe no*
> *sugoki yūgure*

1080 [1674]

> An ancient field
> and in the sole tree starkly
> rising to its side
> sits a dove, calling to its mate:
> the awesome nightfall.

Kubota comments: "Of course there is the motif of a body-piercing lone-liness in such a poem. But its atmosphere is not *dark* in the way we usually use that term. The time of day is undoubtedly nightfall. But, even though the items in front of the poet are becoming indistinguishable from one another, one has no sense here of daytime being pursued and demolished by the night."

This is not to deny, however, that Saigyō's preoccupation with the moon, as shown in the poems of this book, was deep. Yamada Shōzen researched for decades to unearth the multiple and often subtle links between Saigyō's verse and the practices of Buddhism in twelfth-century Japan. He detailed how the use of representations of the full moon or the full moon itself served as the focal point for extended meditations. In these meditations, referred to as *gachirinkan* and prized especially within the Shingon School, the mind/heart *(kokoro)* of the practitioner was visualized as progressively filling with light. Objectives of such exercises included an enhanced ability to recollect the past, greater powers of memorization, and—in the most literal sense— enlightenment. There was even a sense that through such practices something like a personalized luminescent moon would take up residence within the interior of the body-mind of the committed meditator. Yamada suggests that poems otherwise easily mistaken as banal become interesting, even fascinat-ing, when we realize this dimension of Saigyō's preoccupation with the moon. Such meditations explain the frequent occurrence in these poems of the homonym *sumu*. One ideograph for it means "to become lucid" but an alternative denotes "to lodge within." The double entendre catches the way these poems, based on the *gachirinkan,* verbally represent experiences of drawing the moon and its luminosity into the very inner being of the poet-monk. "Residing" there, its light becomes embodied. The following is one such verse:

kumo oō
futakamiyama no
tsukikage wa
kokoro ni sumu ya
miru ni wa aruran   1784

Clouds thickly mantle
these mountains, but the blocked moon

had already taken up residence
in my mind, so nothing now prevents
me from seeing its serenity there.

Saigyō, writes Yamada, inverts the situation with ease. Prevented from viewing the moon in the sky, he finds within himself "what is virtually the same moon."

Konishi summed up this trajectory of research by noting that "Saigyō perceived cherry blossoms and the moon as mandalas" and then went on to caution against judging such poems with only a twentieth-century sensibility and standards, writing that "we must give full consideration to how many people in the twelfth century would have been deeply moved by these poems." This was poetry but it was, at the same time, something more than poetry.

During the very last years of his life, Saigyō composed two *jika-awase*, a new form. In it one poet imagines and writes the poems of two persona, and these write as if in competition *(awase)*. These, the *Mimosusogawa-utaawase* and *Miyagawa-utaawase*, were named after rivers at Ise where Saigyō was living at the time. He sent the first off to Fujiwara Shunzei and the second to Fujiwara Teika (1162–1241) for their opinions. In return he received comments that indicated the high regard the two most eminent court poets had come to have for him. We have reason to think that Shunzei, especially, recognized and valued the *gachirinkan* matrix of Saigyō's poems.

The people who put together the *Shinkokin-shū* early in the thirteenth century seem to have sensed that there was something decidedly new and significant in verse of this type. Out of his large opus—of which more than two thousand are extant—they often selected poems wherein both the poet and the reader can relish the startling beauty in ordinary, almost colorless scenes and events. The poem of Saigyō that over time became best known to the Japanese is precisely such a one:

*kokoro naki
mi ni mo aware wa
shirarekeri
shigi tatsu sawa no
aki no yūgure*   515 [362]

I thought I was free
of passions, so this melancholy
comes as a surprise:
a woodcock shoots up from marsh
where autumn's twilight falls.

Translations of this poem cannot but stumble in trying to render the Japanese word *aware*. With a long history of associations (and often as *mono no aware*) this term, at least for Saigyō, designated the abrupt sense of being confronted with exquisite beauty—but a beauty that, because all things are impermanent, will disappear as quickly as it has arrived. Awe is of its essence. Religious and aesthetic experiences seem to fuse. What makes this poem superb is how Saigyō juxtaposes the subjective experience in the first part of the poem with a swiftly conveyed depiction of an objective, natural event in the second portion. The parts mirror one another. What happens in the scene of the darkening marsh is reflected in the person of the poet, someone in whom, fortunately, long and arduous religious practice had not taken away the capacity to respond emotionally to a sudden manifestation of beauty. That this poem appeared at a time when Saigyō's own life was drawing to a close and locates beauty and composure vis-a-vis twilight of many kinds has, understandably, made it among the most cherished of his compositions.

Saigyō's death, according to the material we have, came suddenly and—in a most literal sense—predictably. At some point well before his actual demise, and probably more than a decade earlier, he had written the following poem. In this verse he alludes to the middle of the second lunar month *(kisaragi)*, thought widely, even if inaccurately, by his contemporaries to have been the calendar date when Shakyamuni entered his complete *nirvana* and died. Saigyō wished for a personal parallel. His poem expressed a vow to die on that calendar date but at the same time in the natural setting—the full moon and cherry trees in bloom—that he had prized throughout his life.

negawaku wa
hana no shita nite
haru shinan
sono kisaragi no
mochizuki no koro   8

Let it be in spring
and under cherry blossoms that
I die, while the moon
is perfect at midmonth, like
it was for his peaceful passing.

The poem appeared in the *Sanka-shū*, a collection most likely done by
Saigyō himself. Since it includes no poems after his move to Ise in 1180, it
appears to have been circulated during the last decade of his life. But this
verse jumped out from all the rest and into the awareness of its readers when
Saigyō, who had been ill and staying at Horokawa-dera, a small Shingon
temple in the area of Osaka, died exactly at the time of year and under the
conditions of nature that he had wanted. The date was the sixteenth of the
second lunar month of 1190.

Shunzei, then the elderly dean of the entire world of court poetry and
someone who shared Saigyō's interest in Buddhism, wrote the following and
put it into his own personal poetry collection, the *Chō-shū eisō:*

negai okishi
hana no moto nite
owarikeri
hachisu no ue mo
tagawazaranan

Just as predicted,
he passed away under
blossoming cherries
and with the same certainty he
now rests on an opened lotus.

Poems treating the way Saigyō's passing matched his prediction were written also by Shunzei's son Teika, fast becoming the most celebrated court poet, and by Jien (1155–1225), a poet, historian, and someone who would eventually become the highest ranking Buddhist prelate of his time.

The precision of Saigyō's prediction went beyond being merely uncanny. The high level of intentionality he had put into the manner of his dying seemed to suggest the same may have been true of his whole life. Ignoring the hestitations, doubts, and struggles evidenced within a number of his poems, hagiographers construed his life story as more single-minded, chaste, and free of cares than it had, in fact, been. The medieval period was developing a growing fascination with paradigmatic figures. The age of the diary about court life and court liaisons was giving way to one in which records, whether real or imagined, of travel to far-flung locations, even if always within Japan, were becoming the preferred literature of the reading classes.

Saigyō was, if we may put it so, ideally suited for such idealization. He *had* traveled, more than once, to distant places. And he left the impression that his own poetry profited from his physical presence at sites where earlier eminent persons had resided or written verse. Others in this new generation now wanted to visit these same semi-sacred locations and profit there from something akin to the inspiration of the muses. That the angst and struggles in Saigyō's life were downplayed so as to focus on him as the enlightened poet par excellence was a process dictated by the dynamics of the time.

This process went fast and far within a mere hundred years. The courtier we have come to know as "Lady Nijō" (1271–?) tells of having been inspired by seeing, at the age of nine, a picture scroll, "Record of the Travels of Saigyō." She also claimed to have taken his life as an ascetic as the model for what she wished to do with her own. The most significant tribute to Saigyō, however, probably came from Bashō, who not only explicitly cited him as the earlier poet he most admired but, with exquisite skill, frequently placed phrases from Saigyō's *waka* into his own poems and travel diaries. It was his own way of ensuring that they would live on.

Poems of Saigyō

toshi kurenu
haru kubeshi to wa
omoine ni
masashiku miete
kanau hatsuyume   1

Closed out the old year
and held a dream of spring behind
my shut eyes...till now
this morning I open them to see
it's really come into the world.

Celebrating spring at each house:

kado goto ni
tatsuru komatsu ni
kazasarete
yado chō yado ni
haru wa kinikeri   6

Gate after gate
adorned with festal pine:
spring has come
to each and every house,
garnishing all with new green.

haru shire to
tani no hosomizu
mori zo kuru
iwama no kōri
hima taenikeri 17

Waking me up
to the spring that's come,
water trickles down
the valley, and long crag-bound ice
now cracks open, slides free.

At the place called Futami ["Two-Views"] in Ise:

nami kosu to
futami no matsu no
mietsuru wa
kozue ni kakaru
kasumi narikeri 20

Look at it one way
and high waves seem to engulf
the pines at Futami,
but then…again…you see
mist masking the treetops.

haru no hodo wa
waga sumu io no
tomo ni narite
furusu na ide so
tani no uguisu   39

Spanning all of spring
as companion for me, another
in a hermit's hut—
don't forsake your nest
here in the valley, warbler!

kumo nakute
oboro nari to mo
miyuru kana
kasumi kakareru
haru no yo no tsuki   61

Clouds dispersed
and still it looks vague,
dreamy up there:
tonight's moon hanging
in the haze of spring.

yamagatsu no
kataoka kakete
shimuru io no
sakai ni tateru
tama no oyanagi   62 [1675]

Penniless woodcutter
managed to get for himself a hut
hanging on a steep slope
and as boundary mark a jewel,
a jade-green young willow tree.

yoshino-yama
kozue no hana o
mishi hi yori
kokoro wa mi ni mo
sowazunariniki   77

Journeying alone:
now my body knows the absence
even of its own heart,
which stayed behind that day when
it saw Yoshino's treetops.

hikikaete
hana miru haru wa
yoru wa naku
tsuki miru aki wa
niru nakaranan   82

In spring I spend day
with flowers, wanting no night;
it's turned around
in fall, when I watch the moon
all night, resenting the day.

hana chirade
tsuki wa kumoran
yo nariseba
mono o omowan
waga mi naramashi   83

A world without
the scattering of blossoms,
without the clouding
over of the moon, would deprive
me of my melancholy.

hana ni somu
kokoro wa ikade
nokoriken
sutehateteki to
omou waga mi ni   87

Why do I, who broke
so completely with this world,
find in my body
still the pulsing of a heart
once dyed in blossoms' hues?

hotoke ni wa
sakura no hana o
tatematsure
waga nochi no yo o
hito toburawaba   89

When gone in death,
I'll take cherry blossoms
as your rite for me…
if any wishes to make memorial here
for me in my life over there.

On seeing an ancient cherry tree with blossoms here and there:

wakite min
oigi wa hana mo
aware nari
ima ikutabi ka
haru ni aubeki   105

I must strain to see
the few buds this old tree
labored to open;
in pathos we're one, and I wonder
how many more springs we'll meet here.

When the blossoms were out at Mountain Temple;
recollections of long ago:

yoshino-yama
hokiji tsutai ni
tazuneirite
hana mishi haru wa
hito mukashi kamo   107

I found my way up
Yoshino's precipice-hung
path and into its
past, seeing there the blossoms
I sought that spring—ages ago.

Having withdrawn from the world, I was on the Eastern Hills
and, at someone's invitation, went to see blossoms at Shirakawa;
but I soon left, reflecting on the past with these words:

chiru o mide
kaeru kokoro ya
sakurabana
mukashi ni kawaru
shirushi naruran 115

This frame of mind
lets me go back, even without
seeing the blossoms fall;
maybe it's some sign I am
no more the one I used to be.

nagamu tote
hana ni mo itaku
narenureba
chiru wakere koso
kanashi kari kere 131

"Detached" observer
of blossoms finds himself in time
intimate with them—
so, when they separate from the branch,
it's he who falls…deeply into grief.

ko no moto ni
tabine o sureba
yoshino-yama
hana no fusuma o
kisuru harukaze   136

Tired from travel,
I'm falling asleep under
a tree at Yoshino
while a spring breeze gathers
and pulls over me a quilt of petals.

kaze sasou
hana no yukue wa
shiranedomo
oshimu kokoro wa
mi ni tomarikeri   145

Seduced by the warm breeze,
my blossoms went off with it
to who-knows-where;
so, loath to lose them, my heart
stays here with nothing but my own self.

harukaze no
hana o chirasu to
miru yume wa
sametemo mune no
sawagu nari keri   150

In my dream I saw
the spring wind gently shaking
blossoms from a tree;
and even now, though I'm awake,
there's motion, trembling in my chest.

iwa tsutai
orade tsutsuji o
te ni zo toru
sakashiki yama no
toridokoro ni wa   184

Scaling the crags
where azalea bloom…not for plucking
but for hanging on!
the saving feature of this rugged
mountain face I'm climbing.

samidare no
harema mo mienu
kumoji yori
yama hototogisu
nakite sugunari 221

Early summer rains:
no let-up, no glimpse of sky,
but somewhere inside
this thick bank of clouds a crying
mountain warbler threads its way.

Finding a cool place in summer at North Shirakawa:

mizu no oto ni
atsusa wasururu
matoi kana
kozue no semi no
koe mo magirete 261

Next to murmuring waters
we're a circle of friends, no longer
minding summer's heat,
and cicada voices in the treetops
mix in well with all the rest.

obotsukana
aki wa ikanaru
yue no areba
suzuro ni mono no
kanashikaruran   321 [367]

All so vague:
the reasons why in autumn
all fall away
and there's just this
inexplicable sadness.

Under the moon, looking far into the distance:

kuma mo naki
tsuki no hikari ni
sasowarete
iku kumoi made
yuku kokoro zo mo   362

So taken with
the faultless face and radiance
of an alluring moon,
my mind goes farther…farther
to reach remote regions of the sky.

oi mo senu
jūgo no toshi mo
aru mono o
koyoi no tsuki no
kakaramashikaba   370

To be just fifteen,
a time without infirmities!
'Tis the moon's age tonight,
as full in the midst of its life,
it's suspended, perfect now.

mushi no ne ni
kareyuku nobe no
kusamura ni
aware o soete
sumeru tsukikage   383

Insect cries more faint
in these clumps of autumn grass
going dry: sympathy
lent this field by shafts
of the moon's light on it.

ko no ma moru
ariake no tsuki o
nagamureba
sabishisa souru
mine no matsukaze   385

Tree-filtered patch
of moonlight fades with dawn;
staring at it gives
loneliness…deepened by winds
soughing through pines on the peaks.

abaretaru
kusa no iori ni
moru tsuki o
sode ni utsushite
nagametsuru kana   388

This leaky, tumbledown
grass hut left an opening for the moon,
and I gazed at it
all the while it was mirrored
in a teardrop fallen on my sleeve.

yukue naku
tsuki ni kokoro no
sumi sumite
hate wa ika ni ka
naran to suran   393

Limitations gone:
since my mind fixed on the moon,
clarity and serenity
make something for which
there's no end in sight.

kumo haruru
arashi no oto wa
matsu ni are ya
tsuki mo midori no
iro ni haetsutsu   402

The clouds dissolved,
but the storm's sound lingering on
in swishing pine boughs
may be why some of the trees' blue
now tints the moon above.

kuma mo naki
tsuki no omote ni
tobu kari no
kage o kumo ka to
magaetsuru kana   406

Not a hint of shadow
on the moon's face...but now
a silhouette passes;
not the cloud I take it for,
but a flock of flying geese.

moro tomo ni
kage o naraburu
hito mo are ya
tsuki no morikuru
sasa no io ni   409

Next to my own
it would be good to have
another's shadow
cast here in the pool of moonlight
leaked into my hut of bamboo grass.

During a journey; concerning the moon:

tsuki wa nao
yo na yo na goto ni
yadorubeshi
waga musubioku
kusa no iori ni   454

As always, the moon
night after night after night
will stay on here
at this grass hut I put together—
and now myself must leave.

With my mind made up to go to worship at Aki Shrine,
I was in a place called Takatomi Cove, where I waited for a gale
to subside. The moon filtered through the reed roof of my hut:

nami no oto o
kokoro ni kakete
akasu kana
toma moru tsuki no
kage o tomo nite   456

Pounding waves are breakers…
of my heart, so I spend the night
in bed with the moon's
light that slips in through
the gaps in my reed hut's roof.

Setting out on a pilgrimage and feeling profound
sentiments with respect to an especially bright moon:

moro tomo ni
tabi naru sora ni
tsuki idete
sumebaya kage no
aware naruran   457

We would together
make the journey, I on land
and it in the sky,
if the moon comes out to stay:
empathy both ways.

miyako nite
tsuki o aware to
omoishi wa
kazu yori hoka no
susabi narikeri   460 [937]

Back in the capital
we gazed at the moon, calling
our feelings "deep"—
mere shallow diversions
that here don't count at all.

Morning; hearing the first geese:

yokogumo no
kaze ni wakaruru
shinonome ni
yama tobikoyuru
hatsu kari no koe   462 [501]

Pushed along by wind,
clouds layered along the peaks
diffuse at daybreak:
honking geese who've crossed
the mountains open the fall.

The voices of geese—far and near:

shirakumo o
tsubasa ni kakete
yuku kari no
kadota no omo no
tomo shitau nari   464 [502]

Wings already wet
by the cold clouds he's entered,
a gander calls out,
yearning for his mate sitting here
in a field just outside my gate.

nagori ōki
mutsugoto tsukide
kaeriyuku
hito o ba kiri mo
tachihedatekeri   468

Lovers' rendezvous
slowly ends with many vows
to let nothing come
between them…then, as he moves off,
rising mists hide him from her.

At a quiet place away from it all; on hearing a deer:

tonari inu
hara no kariya ni
akasu yo wa
shika aware naru
mono ni zo arikeru   481

No other is anywhere
near this borrowed field shed,
so the crying till
daybreak must be a deer's:
alone with all other things.

A ricefield, a hermitage, and a deer:

oyamada no
io chikaku naku
shika no ne ni
odorokasarete
odorokasu kana   482 [448]

Quiet mountain hut
by a rice patch…till a deer's cry
just outside startles me
and I move…so startling him:
we astonish one another!

michi mo nashi
yado wa ko no ha ni
uzumorete
madaki sesasuru
fuyugomori kana   540

All roads disappeared
under thickly fallen leaves,
which buried my place—
completely out of season,
locked in for winter already!

sabishisa ni
taetaru hito no
mata mo are na
iori naraben
fuyu no yamazato   560 [627]

Someone who has learned
how to manage life in loneliness:
would there were one more!
He could winter on this mountain
with his hut right next to mine.

fuyugare no
susamajigenaru
yamazato ni
tsuki no sumu koso
aware narikere   564

Winter has withered
everything in this mountain place:
dignity is in
its desolation now, and beauty
in the cold clarity of its moon.

arachiyama
sakashiku kudaru
tani mo naku
kajiki no michi o
tsukuru shirayuki 577

So steep and dangerous
is Mount Arachi that there's
no path down the valley
till one is made for snowshoes
by white snow fallen over all.

furu yuki ni
shiorishi shiba mo
uzumorete
omowan yama ni
fuyugomorinuru 579

When the fallen snow
buried the twigs bent by me
to mark a return trail,
unplanned, in strange mountains,
I was holed up all winter.

yuki fureba
noji mo yamaji mo
uzumorete
ochikochi shiranu
tabi no sora kana 588

Snow has fallen on
field paths and mountain paths,
burying them all,
and I can't tell here from there:
my journey in the midst of sky.

hitori sumu
katayama kage no
tomo nare ya
arashi ni haruru
fuyu no yo no tsuki 610

Here I huddle, alone,
in a mountain's shadow, needing
some companion somehow:
the cold, biting rains pass off
and give me the winter moon.

Gone far to the northeast; at year's end:

tsune yori mo
kokorobosoku zo
omōyuru
tabi no sora nite
toshi no kurenuru   624

A forlorn feeling,
this time more sharp than ever:
journeying along
under a vast sky where I see
the old year sink to its close.

Passion for a blossom that still has not fallen:

hagakure ni
chiritodomareru
hana nomi zo
shinobishi hito ni
au kokochi suru   653

Hidden away
under leaves, a blossom
still left over
makes me yearn to chance upon
my secret love this way.

Love like cut reeds:

hitokata ni
midaru to mo naki
waga koi ya
kaze sadamaranu
nobe no karu kaya   657

Not so confused
as to lean only one way,
my love life!
A sheaf of field reeds also bends
before each wind that moves it.

Love like fallen leaves:

asa goto ni
koe o osamuru
kaze no oto wa
yo o hete karuru
hito no kokoro ka   660

Each morning the wind
dies down and the rustling leaves
go silent: was this
the passion of all-night lovers
now talked out and parting?

yumihari no
tsuki ni hazurete
mishi kage no
yasashikarishi wa
itsuka wasuremu   683

The crossbow moon is
no longer within my view,
but how could I
forget the sheer loveliness of
its soft shaft of light piercing me?

omokage no
wasurarumajiki
wakare kana
nagori o hito no
tsuki ni todomete   684 [1185]

I'll never forget
her look when I said goodbye…
especially since,
as keepsake, she set her sorrow-
filled face on the moon above.

yoshi saraba
namida no ike ni
mi o nashite
kokoro no mama ni
tsuki o yadosan 697

It will be good:
my body may cry itself into
a pond of tears,
but in it my unchanged heart
will give lodging to the moon.

omokage ni
kimi ga sugata o
mitsuru yori
niwaka ni tsuki no
kumorinuru kana 702

In the portrait
emerging on the moon I spied
your face…so clearly,
the cause of tears, which then
quickly cast the moon in clouds again.

kuma mo naki
ori shi mo hito o
omoidete
kokoro to tsuki o
yatsushitsuru kana 707 [1268]

No pock or shadow
on the moon's face, so just then
I recalled yours—clear—
till tears from my own mind
defaced the moon once more.

tanomoshi na
yoi akatsuki no
kane no oto
monoomou tsumi mo
tsukizarame ya wa 774

Bonging so reliably—
the temple bell heard at dusk
sounds again at dawn…so
will the sins of this whole night
fall from me through its force?

tsukuzuku to
mono o omoi ni
uchisoete
ori aware naru
kane no oto kana   775

In deep reverie
on how time buffets all,
I hear blows fall
on a temple bell…drawing out more
of its sound and my sadness.

noki chikaki
hana tachibana ni
sode shimete
mukashi o shinobu
namida tsutsuman   777

My kimono sleeves,
blossom-scented by the air
under this orange tree
close by the eaves, catch and hold
tears falling from the past's recall.

fukaki yama wa
hito mo toikonu
sumai naru ni
obitadashiki wa
mura zaru no koe

793

Here I've a place
so remote, so mountain-closed,
none comes to call.
But those voices! A whole clan
of monkeys on the way here!

While secluded in a place far away, the moon conveyed my message all
the way back to someone in the capital:

tsuki nomi ya
ue no sora naru
katami nite
omoi mo ideba
kokoro kayowan

795 [1267]

The moon, like you,
is far away from me, but it's
our sole memento:
if you look and recall our past
through it, we can be one mind.

nanigoto ni
tomaru kokoro no
arikereba
sara ni shi mo mata
yo no itowashiki   797 [1831]

When, at this stage
of world-loathing, something captures
the heart, then indeed
the same world is all the more
worthy…of total disdain.

toshitsuki o
ikade waga mi ni
okuriken
kinō no hito mo
kyō wa naki yo ni   836 [1748]

Why, in this world where
one here yesterday is off today
to the world of death,
are more and more years and still
more and more months given me?

On the way to the Tennō-ji Temple, I got caught in the rain. In the area known as Eguchi, I asked at one place for a night's lodging. When refused, I replied as follows:

yo no naka o
itou made koso
katakarame
kari no yadori o
oshimu kimi kana   820 [978]

It is hard, perhaps,
to hate and part with the world;
but you are stingy
even with the night I ask of you,
a place in your soon-left inn.

The response from a "woman of pleasure":

ie o izuru
hito to shi kikeba
kari no yado ni
kokoro tomuna to
omou bakari zo   821 [979]

It's because I heard
you're no longer bound to life
as a householder
that I'm loath to let you get attached
to this inn of brief, bought stays.

Under the moon, recollecting the past:

tsuki o mite
izure no toshi no
aki made ka
kono yo ni ware ga
chigiri aruran   844

That moon up there:
how many more autumns will
I be here to see it?
Something long ago fixed for
this life by an earlier one.

ikade ware
koyoi no tsuki o
mi ni soete
shide no yamaji no
hito o terasamu   845

Drenched here
in moonlight, I hope the dead
too have
this illumination on the paths
they tread through darker worlds.

At a point in time when I was feeling desolate, I heard the voice of a cricket very close to my pillow:

sono ori no
yomogi ga moto no
makura ni mo
kaku koso mushi no
ne ni wa mutsureme   846

At that turning point,
with my head for the last time
pillowed in sagebrush,
I'd have this chirping insect
still be what's closest to me.

My fellow pilgrim [the monk Saijū] had an illness that had reached the critical point; under a bright moon, my sadness:

morotomo ni
nagame nagamete
aki no tsuki
hitori ni naran
koto zo kanashiki   849

Side by side, year
after year, you and I
gazed and gazed
at the autumn moon, which now
seen alone is the sum of sadness.

izuku ni ka
neburi neburite
taorefusan to
omou kanashiki
michibata no tsuyu   916

My body will somewhere fall
by the wayside into a state of
sleep and still more sleep—
like the dew that each night appears,
then falls from roadside grasses.

naki ato o
tare to shiranedo
toribeyama
ono ono sugoki
tsuka no yūgure   920

Nameless remains
go up in smoke here
at Mount Toribe: each one
awesome in its own way—
with night falling on graves.

nami takaki
yo o kogi kogite
hito wa mina
funaoka yama o
tomari ni zo suru   921

The ups and downs of waves
and of a world one maneuvers through—
we're storm-tossed boats,
come at last to final rest
in the pyres on Ship Hill.

shi nite fusamu
koke no mushiro o
omou yori
kanete shiraruru
iwakage no tsuyu   922

My cold corpse
covered forever with moss
for bedding will
recollect what it learned here
from dew on a rock's cold, dark side.

yamanoha ni
kakaruru tsuki o
nagamureba
ware to kokoro no
nishi ni iru kana   942

Staring at the moon
as it dips down and hides itself
on the mountain's other side,
I sense that my own mind goes
willingly toward its own west.

yamakawa no
minagiru mizu no
oto kikeba
semuru inochi zo
omoishiraruru   945

The sound of a swollen
mountain stream rapidly rushing
makes one know
how very quickly life itself
is pressed along its course.

ada naranu
yagate satori ni
kaerikeri
hito no tame ni mo
sutsuru inochi wa 946

Nothing lost…
since in satori everything
thrown away
comes back again: the life
given up for an "other."

madoikite
satori ubeku mo
nakaritsuru
kokoro o shiru wa
kokoro narikeri 947

My dilemma:
that deep realization will
never come to
my mind, the truth of which
my mind realizes all too well.

yami harete
kokoro no sora ni
sumu tsuki wa
nishi no yamabe ya
chikaku naruran   948 [1979]

The mind is a sky
emptied of all darkness,
and its moon,
limpid and perfect, moves
closer to mountains in the west.

On that chapter of the *Lotus Sutra* called "Duration of the Life of the
Tathagata":

washi-no-yama
tsuki o irinu to
miru hito wa
kuraki ni mayou
kokoro nari keri   970

Those who view the moon
over Vulture Peak as one
now sunk below
the horizon…are men whose minds,
confused, hold the real darkness.

[On the nature of] beasts:

kagura uta ni
kusatori kuu wa
ita keredo
nao sono koma ni
naru koto wa ushi   981

Shrine poems
glorify the horses chewing
on grasses there,
although to be born as one
would be a calamity.

no ni tateru
eda naki ko ni mo
otorikeri
nochi no yo shiranu
hito no kokoro wa   989

When a man gives no
mind to what follows this life,
he's worse off than
that tree trunk standing in a field:
no branch or twig anywhere.

izuku ni ka
mi o kakusamashi
itoite mo
ukiyo ni fukaba
yama nakariseba   991

What a wretched place
this would be if this depised,
quickly passing world
had no place to hide away—
that is, no mountains in it.

asaku ideshi
kokoro no mizu ya
tatauran
sumiyuku mama ni
fukaku naru kana   996

The mind for truth
begins, like a stream, shallow
at first, but then
adds more and more depth
while gaining greater clarity.

tou hito mo
omoitaetaru
yamazato no
sabishisa nakuba
sumiukaramashi   1019

Hoped-for, looked-for
guests just never made it to
my mountain hut,
whose congenial loneliness
I'd hate to live without.

mizu no oto wa
sabishiki io no
tomo nare ya
mine no arashi no
taema taema ni   1026

The sound of water
gets to be my sole comfort in
this lonely, battered hut:
in the midst of mountain storm's fury,
drops drip in holes and silences.

tazunekite
kototou hito no
naki yado ni
ko no ma no tsuki no
kage zo sashikuru   1031

This place of mine
never is entered by humans
come for conversation,
only by the mute moon's light shafts
which slip in between the trees.

aware ni zo
monomekashiku wa
kikoekeru
karetaru nara no
shiba no ochiba wa   1046

Patter of pathos:
a sound like falling hailstones,
awesome somehow:
large leaves from the limbs
of an old, now withered, oak.

mase ni saku
hana ni mutsurete
tobu chō no
urayamashiku mo
hakanakari keri　　　　　　　　　　　1112

Now seen...now gone,
the butterfly flits in and out
through fence-hung flowers;
but a life lived so close to them
I envy though it's here and gone.

wabibito no
namida ni nitaru
sakura kana
kaze mi ni shimeba
mazu koboretsutsu　　　　　　　　　　1121

When stung by the world,
man's tears spill drop by drop
like the cherry tree
whose petals scatter down when
whipped by cold winds.

yoshino-yama
yagate ideji to
omou mi o
hana chirinaba to
hito ya matsuran   1122 [1617]

"He'll return," they think,
"when the blossoms all are fallen,"
but he for whom they wait
is thinking now he'll
never leave Mount Yoshino.

ware nare ya
kaze o wazurau
shinodake wa
okifushi mono no
kokorobosokute   1125

We're both afflicted
by drafts and wind, and spend our days
getting up and lying down:
young bamboo weak at its core
and I, ill and disheartened.

After having been on a pilgrimage through many provinces, I was returning to Yoshino in the spring when someone asked me where I would be staying this time; I responded:

hana o mishi
mukashi no kokoro
aratamete
yoshino no sato ni
suman to zo omou 1156

Returning to where
it used to see blossoms,
my mind, changed,
will stay on at Yoshino,
home now, and see anew.

Stopping over at a place called Heichi, I saw the moon while it shone through the treetops and was reflected in drops on my sleeve:

kozue moru
tsuki mo aware o
omou beshi
hikari ni gushite
tsuyu no koboruru 1197

Trickling in through
tree foliage, the moon up there
shows it knows
sadness: in its light here
lies the dew it wept tonight.

I visited someone who had renounced the world and now lives in Saga.
We conversed about the importance for our future lives of daily
and uninterrupted practice of our Buddhist faith. Returned,
I took special notice of an upright shaft of bamboo and wrote this:

yoyo futomo
take no hashira no
hitosuji ni
tatetaru fushi wa
kawarazaranan   1234

Linked worlds,
linked lives: on an
upright shaft
of bamboo, every joint
is strong and straight.

Just as the beams of the sun were retreating before the night,
those of the moon came in through my window:

sashikitsuru
mado no irihi o
aratamete
hikari o kauru
yōzuku yo kana   1241

The sun that shone
in my window now slipped
behind the horizon,
but suddenly light is renewed:
shafts of the moon shine in.

On the [hanging] bridge near the Oku-no-In at Mount Kōya,
the moon was unusually brilliant, and I thought back to that time
when the priest Saijū and I spent a whole night together viewing
the moon from this same bridge. It was just before he left for
the capital, and I will never forget the moon that night.
Now that I am at exactly the same place, I wrote this for him:

kototonaku
kimi koi wataru
hashi no ue ni
arasou mono wa
tsuki no kage nomi   1245

Somehow stretched
from then to now is my love
for you, held on this
bridge of tension between tonight's
moon and the one I saw here with you.

kokoro ni wa
fukaku shimedono
ume no hana
oranu nioi wa
kai nakarikeri   1345

Its sweet scent inhaled
into my inner parts,
but…the plum blossom
when still not plucked off
is still not really mine.

saru hodo no
chigiri wa kimi ni
arinagara
yukanu kokoro no
kurushiki ya na zo   1349

Those promises
made in the past to you
now run up against
this recoiling heart of mine:
suffering lies in the conflict.

kusa no ha ni
aranu tamoto mo
mono omoeba
sode ni tsuyu oki
aki no yūgure   1390

Like grass blades moistened
at their tips with dew,
the sleeves of my robe
are dampened by memories
at nightfall in autumn.

au to mishi
sono yo no yume no
samede arena
nagaki neburi wa
ukarube keredo 1441

That night when we met
to make love in my dreams, I willed
to be a never-awakened one,
though it's said that
everlasting night's a miserable fate.

On seeing a tree that stood in front of my hermitage:

hisa ni hete
waga nochi no yo o
toe yo matsu
ato shinobubeki
hito mo naki mi zo 1449

Long-living pine,
of you I ask: everlasting
services for me and
cover for my corpse; here there's no
human to think of me when gone.

koto o mata
ware sumiukute
ukarenaba
matsu wa hitori ni
naran to suran   1450

If I settle here,
pine, you'll be left again
alone when I
tire of this place and
wander off forever.

kuretake no
fushi shigekaranu
yo nariseba
kono kimi wa tote
sashiidenamashi   1511

Lofty lord,
like bamboo your world has
nodes, knuckles,
complications one on another:
if not so, I'd gladly serve in it.

se o hayami
miyatakegawa o
watariyukeba
kokoro no soko no
sumu kokochi suru   1517

Making my way
through the whirling rapids
of Miyataki River,
I have the sense of being washed
clean to the base of my heart.

nami to miyuru
yuki o wakete zo
kogiwataru
kiso no kakehashi
soko mo mieneba   1523

I push through snow
like white surf on Kiso's
hanging bridge
(gripping rails like oars):
bottom too far below to see.

yoshino-yama
hana no chirinishi
ko no moto ni
tomeshi kokoro wa
ware o matsuran   1544

Yoshino Mountains:
blossoms tumbled to the foot
of trees, fastening
my heart there with them
waiting still for my return.

yoshino-yama
fumoto no taki ni
nagasu hana ya
mine ni tsumorishi
yuki no shitamizu   1552

Yoshino Mountains:
down here it is cascades of
water spread with
white petals; up there on the peaks
it starts out running under deep snow.

nanigoto ka
kono yo ni hetaru
omoide o
toekashi hito ni
tsuki o oshien 1570

To that person
wanting recall of events past
in this world below:
"Why not ask the moon above?"
may be the most fit response.

kimi o ikade
komaka ni yueru
shigeme yui
tachi mo hararezu
narabitsutsu min 1587

On you somehow
the close weave of that fine
fabric will not come
undone; would I were so close,
myself interwoven with you.

sasagani no
ito ni tsuranuku
tsuyu no tama o
kakete kazareru
yo ni koso arikere   1605

Delicate dewdrops
on a spider's web are the pearls
strung on necklaces
worn in the world man spins:
a world quickly vanishing.

utsutsu o mo
utsutsu to sara ni
oboeneba
yume o mo yume to
nanika omowan   1606

Since the "real world" seems
to be less than truly real,
why need I suppose
the world of dreams is nothing
other than a world of dreams?

tomoshibi no
kakage chikara mo
nakunarite
tomaru hikari o
matsu waga mi kana   1608

Strength to lift
up the flickering lamp
has dissipated;
now all of me looks to
the end of this light.

yo no naka ni
nakunaru hito o
kiku tabi ni
omoi wa shiru o
orokanaru mi ni   1613

People pass away
and the truth of the passing world
impresses me
now and then…but otherwise my dull
wits let this truth too pass away.

On that chapter of the *Lotus Sutra* entitled "A Peaceful Life," especially on the phrase "Entering deeply into meditation and seeing buddhahood in all ten directions":

fukaki yama ni
kokoro no tsuki shi
suminureba
kagami ni yomo no
satori o zo miru   1658

In the mountains' deep
places, the moon of the mind
resides in light serene:
moon mirrors all things everywhere,
mind mirrors moon...in *satori* now.

tomekokashi
ume sakari naru
waga yado o
utoki mo hito wa
ori ni koso yore   1693 [51]

Now's the time to visit:
Just when my place is full of
opened plum blossoms!
Long unseen humans too wait for
just the right time to come forth.

fukenikeru
waga mi no kage o
omou ma ni
haruka ni tsuki no
katabukinikeru   1741 [1534]

While noticing how time
has bent my body's silhouette
cast in the moonlight...
away off in the distance the moon
sank closer to the world's rim.

haru goto no
hana ni kokoro o
nagusamete
musoji amari no
toshi o henikeru   1775

Each and every spring,
blossoms gave my mind its
comfort and pleasure:
now more than sixty years
have gone by like this.

omoiide ni
hana no nami ni mo
nagareba ya
mine no shirakumo
taki kudasumeri   1828

If only I could
float along on a surf of blossoms—
I recall so well
how they poured down from the heights
like a cascade of white cloud.

yoshino-yama
oku o ware zo
shirinubeki
hana yue fukaku
irinaraitsutsu   1830

Yoshino Mountains—
the one who will get to know
you inside-out is I,
for I've gotten used to going
into your depths for blossoms.

furizu na o
suzuka ni naruru
yamadachi wa
kikoetataki mo
toridokoro ka na   1840

Notorious
mountain robber lies
on Mount Deer-bell,
picked apart himself now
by noisy raptor birds.

A Sequence of Poems
On Looking at Pictures of Hell

miru mo ushi
ika ni ka subeki
waga kokoro
kakaru mukui no
tsumi ya arikeru   1841

I am in pain just
looking at these scenes;
what does this mean for me?
That this mental torture springs
from heinous things I once pursued?

ukegataki
hito no sugata ni
ukamiide
korizu ya dare mo
mata shizumubeki   1844

Surfacing as a human
is a hard-won achievement,
but submerging, slipping
down again, is so easy that
anyone anytime can do it.

kurogane no
tsume no tsurugi no
hayakimote
katami ni mi o mo
houru kanashisa   1846

Swords studded
with metal clawhooks
are gruesomely
designed for hacking off
half of another's body.

omoki iwa o
momo hirochihiro
kasane agete
kudakuya nani no
mukui naruran   1847

A body crushed
under monstrous rocks reaching
a whole mile up:
for what high crime is this,
one wonders, the fit reward?

In what is called the Hell of Black Ropes, bodies are hewn:

tsumibito wa
shide no yamaba no
somagi kana
ono no tsurugi ni
mi o wararetsutsu   1848

Death mountain
is a lumberyard of sinners:
blades and saws
tear up their bodies,
slice by slice by slice.

hitotsu mi o
amata ni kaze no
fukikirite
homuru ni nasu mo
kanashikarikeri   1849

One body cut up
and spread around can itself
become fuel for
big blazes where the sorrows
of the many are hellish.

nani yori mo
shita nuku ku koso
kanashikere
omou koto o mo
iwaseji no hata   1850

The peculiar pain
of having the tongue torn out
lies in inability
to cry out the nature
of such punishment.

In the place where men are burned in black flames:

nabete naki
kuroki homura no
kurushimi wa
yoru no omohi no
mukui narikeri   1851

Black fires had
their origin in dark nights
of raging passion;
stygian flame is surely
like no other.

aware mishi
chibusa no koto mo
wasurekeri
waga kanashimi no
ku nomi oboeru   1854

It leaves everything
to be desired—the forgetting
of mother's breasts;
recognizing this, I see
my longing as pain.

asahi ni ya
musubu kōri no
ku wa tokemu
mutsu no wa o kiku
akatsuki no sora   1867

Morning's sun
loosens the hard ice;
so the sound of a staff
signals rescue by Jizō
from the cycle of rebirth.

yoshino-yama
kozo no shiori no
michi kaete
mada minukata no
hana o tazunen   1883 [86]

Last year, Yoshino,
I walked away bending branches
to point me to blossoms—
which now are everywhere, and I can
go where I've never been before.

Taira no Tadamori [1095–1153] sponsored a gathering of monks from Mount Kōya at the place where he summered at the springs of Eighth Avenue. I was among the monks who did a ritual service in conjunction with the making of a Buddhist picture there. The moon was bright and, hearing the croaking of frogs, I composed this poem:

saya fukete
tsuki ni kawazu no
koe kikeba
migiwa mo suzushi
ike no ukikusa   1937

The night deepens
and moonlight spreads
a coolness to the edges
of the pond, with fronds on
its surface and a frog's voice.

iwama tojishi
kōri mo kesa wa
tokesomete
koke no shitamizu
michi motomuran   1939 [7]

Tightly held by rocks
through winter, the ice today
begins to come undone:
a way-seeker also is the water,
melting, murmuring from the moss.

yoshino-yama
sakura ga eda ni
yuki chirite
hana osogenaru
toshi ni mo aru kana   1950 [79]

Yoshino Mountain:
white puffs on cherry limbs
are fallen snow,
informing me that blossoms
will be late this year.

sakisomuru
hana o hito eda
mazu orite
mukashi no hito no
tame to omowan   1955

The first sprig just
breaking into bloom:
what if I would snap it off
and use it as memorial
for someone torn away from me?

omoikaesu
satori ya kyō wa
nakaramashi
hana ni someoku
iro nakariseba   1956

Today's satori:
such a change of mind would
not exist without
my lifelong habit of having
my mind immersed in blossoms.

haru o hete
hana no sakari ni
aikitsutsu
omoide ōki
waga mi narikeri   1958

For many springs
I've come here to meet
and unite my mind
with the opening blossoms—so
I'm made of many recollections.

michinobe no
shimizu nagaruru
yanagi kage
shibashi tote koso
tachidomaritsure   2005 [262]

"Just a brief stop,"
I said when stepping off the road
into a willow's shade
where a bubbling stream flows by,
as has time since my "brief stop" began.

yoraretsuru
nomose no kusa no
kageroite
suzushiku kumoru
yūdachi no sora   2007 [263]

Curling in the heat
this small field's grass blades
now find shelter
under cooling clouds: night falls
with rain from the vast sky.

aware ika ni
kusaba no tsuyu no
koboruran
akikaze tachinu
miyagino no hara   2012 [300]

One is moved by
dewdrops hanging from
grass blades and
now facing fall's fierce wind:
on the wide heath at Miyagino.

tsuki miba to
chigiri okite shi
furusato no
hito mo ya koyoi
sode nurasuran   2021 [938]

Tonight's moon stirs
memory of a pact to let
it do this to us:
maybe she, back where we loved,
has tear-wet sleeves like mine.

komu yo ni wa
kokoro no uchi ni
arawasan
akade yaminuru
tsuki no hikari o   2036

Beyond this life and
this world I'll have it till
my heart's content:
the bright moon that passed over
the horizon before I had my fill.

hito wa kode
kaze no keshiki mo
fukenuru ni
aware ni kari no
otozurete yuku   2042 [1200]

The one expected
doesn't come, and the moaning wind
tells the night is late;
a sound outside deepens loneliness:
geese, calling, fly past.

kirigirisu
yozamu ni aki no
naru mama ni
yowaru ka koe no
tōzakari yuku   2051 [472]

As each night of fall
grows colder than the one before,
the chirp of the cricket
gets more feeble: each night it
moves farther into the distance.

tsuki o matsu
takane no kumo wa
harenikeri
kokoro arubeki
hatsushigure kana   2053 [246]

In early winter's rain
I'm pleased when up at the peak
clouds spread open
to show me the moon I longed to see:
a storm that knows compassion.

A winter poem:

yamagawa ni
hitori hanarete
sumu oshi no
kokoro shiraruru
nami no ue kana   2063 [1193]

On a mountain stream,
a mandarin duck made single
by loss of its mate
now floats quietly over ripples:
a frame of mind I know.

ariake wa
omoide are ya
yokogumo no
tadayowaretsuru
shinonome no sora   2080 [1193]

The moon as dawn breaks
glides freely through thick clouds,
layer on layer:
then strata of the past as well,
one by one, open before my mind.

kore ya mishi
mukashi sumiken
ato naran
yomogi ga tsuyu ni
tsuki no yadoreru   2097 [1680]

Can it be just this
that remains of my earlier
stay here:
the moon dwelling in a dewdrop
hung on wormwood in a waste?

At the time when the priest Jakunen invited others to contribute verses
to a hundred-poem collection, I declined to take part. But then on the
road while making a pilgrimage to Kumano, I had a dream. In it
appeared Tankai, the administrator of Kumano, and [the poet]
Shunzei. Tankai said to Shunzei: "Although all things in this world
undergo change, the way of poetry extends unaltered even to the last
age." I opened my eyes and understood. Then I quickly wrote a verse
and sent it off to Jakunen. This is what I composed there in the heart
of the mountains:

sue no yo no
kono nasake nomi
kawarazu to
mishi yume nakuba
yoso ni kikamashi   2103 [1844]

"Even in an age
gone bad the lyric's way
stays straight"—
not seeing this in a dream,
I'd have been deaf to truth.

Seeing the moon at Tsukiyomi Shrine [at Ise]:

sayaka naru
washi no takane no
kumoi yori
kage yawaraguru
tsukiyomi no mori   2123 [1879]

Over Vulture Peak
there in Buddha's time and place:
a bedazzling moon,
here softly filtered into
Tsukiyomi sacred shrine.

tsu no kuni no
naniwa no haru wa
yume nare ya
ashi no kareba ni
kaze wataruru nari   2157 [625]

Famed for its springtime,
Naniwa in Tsu, seen today at last:
a field of withered reeds
bent down by harsh winds—my dream
to see it come false…come true.

yama fukaku
sakoso kokoro wa
kayou tomo
sumade aware o
shiran mono kawa   2161 [1630]

By imagining
these mountain depths, some might think
they come and go here;
but, not living here themselves,
can they know true pathos?

yamazato ni
ukiyo itowan
hito mo gana
kuyashiku sugishi
mukashi kataran   2170 [1657]

Here in these mountains
I'd like one other who turned
his back to the world:
we'd go on about the useless way
we spent our days when in society.

mukashi mishi
niwa no komatsu ni
toshi furite
arashi no oto o
kozue ni zo kiku   2172 [1677]

A garden sapling
when long ago I saw this pine—
now so grown, its high
branches in their soughing say
time goes and a storm comes.

izuku ni mo
sumarezuba tada
sumade aran
shiba no iori no
shibashi naru yo ni   2175 [1778]

Nowhere is there place
to stop and live, so only
everywhere will do:
each and every grass-made hut soon leaves
its place within this withering world.

hana sakishi
tsuru no hayashi no
sono kami o
yoshino no yama no
kumo ni mishi kana 2186

I saw in Yoshino's
billows of blossoms that long-ago
time of great passing
when the *sala* trees surrounding him
suddenly turned as white as cranes.

Page of text:

1. **Bashō…named Saigyō.** Matsuo Bashō 1967: 71.

1–2. **"Bashō traveled dressed in borrowed clerical robes."** Bashō's travels are mapped with precision in Collcutt, Jansen, and Kumakura 1988: 156, a work that provides a wealth of maps and other materials about every era of Japanese history.

2. **less "aesthetic distance."** Brower and Miner 1961: 300.

5. **"exceptional ability in *kemari.*"** Mezaki 1978: 20.

7. **scare quotes around the term "retirement."** The important work's on this and related topics are Hurst 1976 and Hurst 1999.

9. **"Within the hidden side of the culture."** Mezaki 1988: 12.

9. **Gomi Fumihiko.** Gomi 1984: 416–38.

9. **"Erotic love between males and females."** Mezaki 1988: 13. Palaces and monasteries differed in this regard. As now amply documented in translations by Margaret Childs, the "*Chigo Kannon Engi* and other literary sources reveal that in medieval Japan there was a deep ambivalence among monks regarding the applicability of the precept that forbade all sexual activity to intimate relations between men." Childs 1996: 31.

10. **Kubota notes.** Kubota 1983: 68ff.

15. **hagiographic *Tale of Saigyō.*** See Heldt 1997, McKinney 1998, and LaFleur 1976.

17. **physical fighting between bands of monks.** See Weinstein 1999: 489–97.

19. **the struggle with his internal demons.** Kubota 1983: 112–13.

21. **emulate the sufferings of beings.** Kubota 1988: 89.

23. **Nōin may have never gone.** On the reasons why this question has fascinated scholars right up to the present day, see Kamens 1997: 151–54.

24. **Fujiwara Sanekata.** Kamens 1997: 29 explains why the location of Sanekata's exile came to have poetic associations. Bashō, aware of Saigyō's stop there, attempted the same. See Matsuo Bashō 1967: 110.

27ff. On events leading up to the Hōgen Disturbance, see Hurst 1976: 154–77 and Hurst 1999: 576–643.

28. *mi o sutsuru.* The version of the poem cited here is that of the imperial anthology and is taken from Matsuno 1988: 104. A slightly different version in the *Sanka-shū* is number 2169.

29. **"A poem such as this."** Kobayashi 1951: 21.

31. **three and a half centuries.** Hurst 1999: 690.

31. **"To the courtiers in the capital."** Kubota 1961: 203.

33. *Hōgen Monogatari.* Wilson 1971: 99.

34. **resentful and restless spirit.** The paradigmatic case of disorder thought to be caused by a resentful spirit is presented in Borgen 1986.

34. **"As in the case of all unsettled."** Hurst 1976: 207.

34. **In either case, this verse…importance.** Mezaki 1978: 229–35 and Kubota 1973: 70–72.

35. **six tiers of existence.** See LaFleur 1983: 29–59.

35ff. Saigyō's connection to Kūkai is looked at in detail in Yamada 1987.

36. **in a mode of visual and mental play.** On *samadhi* as play, see LaFleur 1983: 54–59.

38. **hardly something to the taste of most courtiers.** Noting how innovative these subjects were, Konishi writes: "These are subjects never before treated in *waka.*" Konishi 1991: 75.

39. **Kubota is dissatisfied.** Kubota 1973: 72–75.

41ff. On Taira Kiyomori, see especially Hurst 1999: 616–32.

43. **Saigyō, much more ready than his fellow poets.** Kubota 1961: 339.

44. **fought near the famous bridge at Uji.** See Farris 1992: 291.

45. **some of the royal regalia.** These purportedly were the sacred jewel and the sacred sword. See translation in Kitagawa and Tsuchida 1975, vol. 2: 676–77.

46. **sentiments of a dutiful son.** Takagi is among those scholars who, in her study of the religious dimension in Saigyō, sees a veiled reference here to something shameful about the death of the poet's father. Takagi 1988: 197.

47. **The specific kind of picture.** For more on the "tree of swords," see LaFleur 2002.

51. **Arakida family…interest in Buddhism.** Kubota 1988: 174.

51. **Allan Grapard rightly points out.** Grapard 1992: 74–75.

52. *honji-suijaku.* For more on this topic, see Sanford et al. 1992.

53. **a form of Buddhist *mantra*.** Abe 1999: 3–5.

56. **"Although some courtiers were still."** Adolphson 2000: 165.

56. **"To people living in the age of *mappō*."** Varley 1994: 112.

58. **"why have I begun."** Rodd 1984: 219.

61. *Azuma Kagami.* The section I translate here is located in Kuroita 1931: 240.

64. **"oh sweet yearning."** Rodd 1984: 249.

64. **"Even when physically at a distance."** Kubota 1973: 169.

65. **"a sense that even poor, frost-wasted."** Miner 1968: 112.

65. **"Saigyō is important because."** Miner 1968: 105.

66. **"Of course there is the motif."** Kubota 1973: 166.

67. **Saigyō, writes Yamada, inverts the situation with ease.** Yamada 1987: 27 and 214–15. He also points out that *futakamiyama* is not necessarily a place name. I share his view that the notion of "metaphor" does not grasp the degree of identification—between the moon and the mind, for instance—aimed at in these Buddhist practices. Manaka 1972: 172ff. may be the earliest treatment of *gachirinkan* and literature.

67. **Konishi summed up this trajectory.** Konishi 1991: 83 and 85.

70. **Poems treating the way Saigyō's passing.** In her valuable study, Hartwieg-Hiratsuka 1984: espec. 62ff. demonstrates how these verses became part of the medieval trajectory of honoring and idealizing Saigyō.

70. **"Lady Nijō."** See Brazell 1973: 52, but also Konishi 1991: 474–75 for the reasons why this may be fictive. That such a scroll was in existence by the time she wrote her "diary," however, seems certain.

70. **frequently placed phrases from Saigyō's *waka*.** For an example of this, see LaFleur 1983: 149–64.

Notes to the poems:

84. **So taken with/ the faultless face.** Begun with words that hint that the moon is like the adored face of a lover, this poem exemplifies Saigyō's ability to transform it, as Konishi suggests, into a mandala in nature and, thus, a link to infinity.

99. **I'll never forget/ her look.** It needs to be remembered that the original in love poems such as this does not specify gender. Conventions of the time assumed, perhaps not always with accuracy, that the recipient was of the other gender.

105. **It is hard, perhaps.** This poem and response in verse that follow are ones in which Saigyō portrays himself asking for shelter at residence of a prostitute and receiving back not only a refusal but a little homily. This pair of poems was selected for inclusion in the *Shinkokin-shū* and eventually became the theme for a famous Noh play, *Eguchi,* whose original was drafted by Kan'ami but was substantively improved by Zeami. Tyler 1992: 68–81 translates it. How this prostitute was later viewed as a bodhisattva is discussed in LaFleur 1983: 69–74.

112. **Those who view the moon.** "Vulture Peak" was the accepted name for the somewhat elevated ground on which, according to tradition, Shakyamuni stood to preach what became the text known popularly in East Asia as the *Lotus Sutra.* In this poem Saigyō appears to be offering a criticism of persons who held that, since the world had entered into the period of the "final dharma" *(mappō),* the practice of Buddhism had become virtually impossible. See also poem number 2123 below.

118. **"He'll return," they think.** On this verse Konishi astutely comments: "Those who know the speaker's attachment to cherry blossoms might be thinking (or saying) that he will leave Mount Yoshino once the blossoms have fallen. But the speaker has no desire to leave then, because he can still see the blossoms' beauty in his mind and remains spellbound by a vision transcending the actual blossoms…. This may be why Saigyō is said to have written poetry of 'unusually deep feeling.'" Konishi 1991: 74.

128. **Since the "real world" seems.** Even in the West, persons familiar with Chinese texts see a hint of Chuang Tzu unable or unwilling to know whether he is dreaming of being a butterfly or vice versa. Within the world of Japanese Buddhists, it was common to see dreams as raising this kind of question. See LaFleur 1983: 1–9.

139. **Morning's sun/ loosens the hard ice.** Although this verse does not explicitly mention the bodhisatta Jizō, a reference in it to "hearing the sound of the staff of six rings" *(mutsu no wa o kiku)* makes things clear. Jizō, who traditionally was assumed capable of rescuing sentient beings from suffering in the six realms of existence *(rokudō),* carried a staff topped by six rings. Anyone hearing their sound knew salvation was on the way.

148. **Even in an age/ gone bad.** See LaFleur 1983: 2–9 for a discussion of this poem. Note too the kinesthetic elements in it.

150. **By imagining/ these mountain depths, some might think.** Here Saigyō expresses doubts about the ability of his urban contemporaries, if they never try living in mountains, to grasp *aware* or *mono no aware,* the profound beauty in things, precisely *because* they are impermanent.

Bibliography

Abe, Ryūichi. 1999. *The Weaving of Mantra: Kūkai and the Construction of Esoteric Buddhist Discourse.* New York: Columbia University Press.

Adolphson, Mikael S. 2000. *The Gates of Power: Monks, Courtiers, and Warriors in Premodern Japan.* Honolulu: University of Hawaii Press.

Borgen, Robert. 1986. *Sugawara Michizane and the Early Heian Court.* Cambridge MA: Harvard University Press.

Brazell, Karen, trans. 1973. *The Confessions of Lady Nijō.* Stanford: Stanford University Press.

Brower, Robert H. and Earl Miner. 1961. *Japanese Court Poetry.* Stanford: Stanford University Press.

Childs, Margaret H., trans. 1996. "The Story of Kannon's Manifestation as a Youth" and "The Tale of Genmu" in Stephen D. Miller, ed., *Partings at Dawn: An Anthology of Japanese Gay Literature.* San Francisco: Gay Sunshine Press, pp. 31–54.

Collcutt, Martin, Marius Jansen, and Isao Kumakura. 1988. *Cultural Atlas of Japan.* New York: Facts on File Publications.

Farris, William Wayne. 1992. *Heavenly Warriors: The Evolution of Japan's Military, 500–1300.* Cambridge MA: Harvard University Press.

Friday, Karl F. 1992. *Hired Swords: The Rise of Private Warrior Power in Early Japan.* Stanford: Stanford University Press.

Gomi Fumihiko. 1984. *Inseiki shakai no kenkyū.* Tokyo: Yamakawa shuppansha.

Grapard, Allan G. 1992. *The Protocol of the Gods: A Study of the Kasuga Cult in Japanese History.* Berkeley: University of California Press.

Hartwieg-Hiratsuka, Keiko. 1984. *Saigyō-Rezeption: Das von Saigyō verkörperte Eremiten-Ideal in der japanischen Literaturgeschichte.* Bern: Peter Lang.

Heldt, Gustav, trans. 1997. "Saigyō's Traveling Tale: A Translation of *Saigyō Monogatari.*" *Monumenta Nipponica* 52:4, pp. 467–521.

Hurst, G. Cameron III. 1976. *Insei: Abdicated Sovereigns in the Politics of Late Heian Japan, 1086–1185.* New York: Columbia University Press.

Hurst, G. Cameron III. 1999. *"Insei"* in Donald H. Shively and William H. McCullough, eds., *The Cambridge History of Japan. Volume 2: Heian Japan.* Cambridge: Cambridge University Press, pp. 576–643.

Ishida, Yoshisada. 1960. *Shinkokinwaka-shū zenchūkai.* Tokyo: Yūseidō shuppan.

Itō Yoshio, ed. 1947. *Sanka-shū.* Tokyo: Asahi shimbunsha.

Kamens, Edward. 1997. *Utamakura, Allusion, and Intertextuality in Traditional Japanese Poetry.* New Haven: Yale University Press.

Kitagawa, Hiroshi and Bruce T. Tsuchida, trans. 1975. *The Tale of the Heike,* 2 vols. Tokyo: University of Tokyo Press.

Kobayashi Hideo. 1951. "Saigyō," as republished in Mezaki Tokue, ed., *Shisō tokuhon: Saigyō.* Kyoto: Hōzōkan, 1984: 18–29.

Konishi Jin'ichi. 1991. *A History of Japanese Literature: Volume Three: The High Middle Ages.* Trans. by Aileen Gatten and Mark Harbison. Princeton: Princeton University Press.

Kubota Jun. 1973. *Shinkokin kajin no kenkyū.* Tokyo: Tōkyō daigaku shuppankai.

———. 1982. *Saigyō zenshū.* Tokyo: Nihon koten bungakkai.

———. 1983. *Koten o yomu: Sankashū.* Tokyo: Iwanami shoten.

———. 1988. *Saigyō no sekai.* Tokyo: Nihon hōsō shuppan.

———. 1996. *Sōan to tabiji utau: Saigyō.* Tokyo: Shintensha.

Kubota Shōichirō. 1961. *Saigyō no kenkyū.* Tokyo: Tōkyōdō shuppan.

Kuroita Katsumi, ed. 1931. *Azuma Kagami* vol. 36. Tokyo: Yoshikawa kōbunkan.

LaFleur, William R. 1976. "The Death and the 'Lives' of Saigyō: The Genesis of a Buddhist Sacred Biography," in Frank E. Reynolds and Donald Capps, eds., *The Biographical Process.* The Hague: Mouton, pp. 343–61.

———, trans. 1978. *Mirror for the Moon: A Selection of Poems by Saigyō (1118–1190).* New York: New Directions.

———. 1983. *The Karma of Words: Buddhism and the Literary Arts in Medieval Japan.* Berkeley: University of California Press.

———. 2002. "Vegetation from Hell: Blossoms, Sex, Leaves, and Blades in

Ominameshi," in Mae Smethurst, ed., *Ominameshi: A Flower in Noh Viewed from Many Directions.* Ithaca: Cornell University Press.

Manaka Fujiko. 1972. *Kokubungaku ni sesshu sareta bukkyō.* Tokyo: Bun'ichi shuppan.

Matsuno Yōichi, ed. 1988. *Shikawaka-shū.* Osaka: Izumi shoin.

Matsuo Bashō. 1967. *The Narrow Road to the Deep North and Other Travel Sketches.* Trans. by Nobuyuki Yuasa. New York: Viking Peguin.

McKinney, Meredith, trans. 1998. *The Tale of Saigyō.* Ann Arbor: University of Michigan Center for Japanese Studies.

Mezaki Tokue. 1978. *Saigyō no shisōshiteki kenkyū.* Tokyo: Yoshikawa kōbunkan.

———. 1988. *Suki to mujō.* Tokyo: Yoshikawa kōbunkan.

Miner, Earl. 1968. *An Introduction to Japanese Court Poetry.* Stanford: Stanford University Press.

Rodd, Laurel Rasplica, trans. 1984. *Kokinshū: A Collection of Poems Ancient and Modern.* Princeton: Princeton University Press.

Sanford, James H., William R. LaFleur, and Masatoshi Nagatomi, eds. 1992. *Flowing Traces: Buddhism in the Literary and Visual Arts of Japan.* Princeton: Princeton University Press.

Takagi, Kiyoko. 1988. *Saigyō no shūkyōteki sekai.* Tokyo: Ōmyōdō.

Tyler, Royall, trans. 1992. *Japanese Nō Dramas.* New York: Penguin.

Varley, Paul. 1994. *Warriors of Japan as Portrayed in the War Tales.* Honolulu: University of Hawaii Press.

Watanabe, Tamotsu. 1971. *Saigyō Sanka-shū zenchūkai.* Tokyo: Kazama shobō.

Watson, Burton, trans. 1991. *Saigyo: Poems of a Mountain Home.* New York: Columbia University Press.

Weinstein, Stanley. 1999. "Aristocratic Buddhism," in Donald H. Shively and William H. McCullough, eds., *The Cambridge History of Japan, Volume 2: Heian Japan.* Cambridge: Cambridge University Press, pp. 489–516.

Wilson, William R., trans. 1971. *Hōgen Monogatari: Tale of Disorder in Hōgen.* Tokyo: Sophia University.

Yamada Shōzen. 1987. *Saigyō no waka to bukkyō.* Tokyo: Meiji shoin.

Index of First Lines

Index

About the Author

If Saigyō found himself journeying over the same difficult mountain road a second time after many decades (p. 57), William R. (Bill) LaFleur finds himself negotiating his way over the terrain of Saigyō's wonderful poetry again after many years. His *Mirror for the Moon: A Selection of Poems by Saigyō* (New Directions) was published way back in 1978. During the intervening years he wrote books such as *The Karma of Words: Buddhism and the Literary Arts in Medieval Japan* (California 1983), *Liquid Life: Abortion and Buddhism in Japan* (Princeton 1992), and edited *Dōgen Studies* (Hawaii 1985) and Masao Abe's widely read *Zen and Western Thought* (Macmillan/Hawaii 1985). More recently he has been studying bioethics in Japan, especially how that nation's religious and philosophical traditions make for perspectives different from those common in North America. A book on that topic may show up soon. Returning to Saigyō to write *Awesome Nightfall,* however, has been the realization of a long-held dream.

Bill is the E. Dale Saunders Professor in Japanese Studies at the University of Pennsylvania. Various fellowships as well as the Watsuji Tetsurō Culture Prize in Japan have greatly benefited his work. He lives not far from Philadelphia with his wife, Mariko, his youngest child, Kiyomi, their sweet chocolate lab Hannya, his cello, his vegetable garden (often on sabbatical), and a zen cushion (also too often on sabbatical). The pleasure of having fine students—at Princeton, UCLA, and now Penn—helped much to make life as a scholar-teacher a very satisfying one. From time to time he publishes his own poems, and these, he hopes, will some day comprise a volume of their own.

Wisdom Publications

Wisdom Publications is a nonprofit publisher, is dedicated to making available authentic works relating to Buddhism for the benefit of all. We publish books by ancient and modern masters in all traditions of Buddhism, translations of important texts, and original scholarship. Additionally, we offer books that explore East-West themes unfolding as traditional Buddhism encounters our modern culture in all its aspects. Our titles are published with the appreciation of Buddhism as a living philosophy, and with the special commitment to preserve and transmit important works from Buddhism's many traditions.

To learn more about Wisdom, or to browse books online, visit our website at www.wisdompubs.org.

You may request a copy of our catalog online or by writing to this address:

Wisdom Publications
199 Elm Street
Somerville, Massachusetts 02144 USA
Telephone: 617-776-7416
Fax: 617-776-7841
Email: info@wisdompubs.org
www.wisdompubs.org

The Wisdom Trust

As a nonprofit publisher, Wisdom is dedicated to the publication of Dharma books for the benefit of all sentient beings and dependent upon the kindness and generosity of sponsors in order to do so. If you would like to make a donation to Wisdom, you may do so through our website or our Somerville office. If you would like to help sponsor the publication of a book, please write or email us at the address above.

Thank you.

Wisdom is a nonprofit, charitable 501(c)(3) organization affiliated with the Foundation for the Preservation of the Mahayana Tradition (FPMT).

Daughters of Emptiness
Poems by Buddhist Nuns of China
Beata Grant
256 pp, ISBN 0-86171-362-1, $16.95

"A landmark collection of exquisite poems scrupulously gathered and translated by Beata Grant. Grant provides an impressively compact and readable overview of the changing fortunes of Buddhist nuns in China, beginning in the fourth century, all the way to the present."—*Buddhadharma: The Practitioner's Quarterly*

"I gratefully await further publications from this talented and dedicated scholar."—Grace Schireson, in *Turning Wheel*

Everything Yearned For
Manhae's Poems of Love and Longing
Translated & introduced by Francisca Cho
144 pp, cloth, ISBN 0-86171-489-X, $15.00

Winner of the Daesan Foundation Literary Award.

"Francisca Cho has provided the definitive English translation of these remarkable poems. Manhae's long rhythmical lines seem to sweep forward with an almost Biblical cadence in some places, while in others breaking apart into brief, almost conversational phrases. Their mix of the philophical, mystical, and sensual are uniquely distinctive. A wonderful voyage awaits you."—from the foreword by David R. McCann, recipient of the Manhae Prize for Arts and Sciences, and Director of the Korea Institute at Harvard University

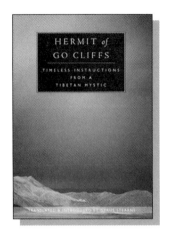

Hermit of Go Cliffs
Timeless Instructions from a Tibetan Mystic
Translated and introduced by
Cyrus Stearns
224 pp, ISBN 0-86171-164-5, $19.95

"An inspiring collection and an exceptional resource."—Janet Gyatso, Harvard University

"A valuable new addition to the still small body of scholarship and translation clarifying the formation of Tibetan Buddhist thought and practice during the crucial period from the eleventh through thirteenth centuries."—Matthew Kapstein, University of Chicago

The Splendor of an Autumn Moon
The Devotional Verse of Tsongkhapa
Translated by Gavin Kilty
224 pages, ISBN 0-86171-192-0, $16.95

Here, presented in both the original Tibetan and in English translation, are twenty-one devotional poems by the Tibetan saint Tsongkhapa (1357–1419), the founder of the Dalai Lama's tradition of Tibetan Buddhism. Gavin Kilty's commentary places each prayer into context, and his translations are absolutely artful.

"Some of the most inspiring verses ever written."—Geshe Thupten Jinpa, Ph.D., founder of the Institute for Tibetan Classics

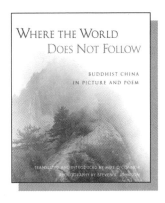

Where the World Does Not Follow
Buddhist China in Picture and Poem
Translated and introduced by Mike O'Connor
Photography by Steven R. Johnson
Foreword by William Neill
128 pp, ISBN 0-86171-309-5, $24.95

"The genius of this book is the timelessness that emerges from juxtaposing modern photographs with T'ang Dynasty Buddhist poetry. The photos or the poetry alone would make this a wonderful text. The two together are something truly special."—*Shambhala Sun*

When I Find You Again It Will Be in Mountains
The Selected Poems of Chia Tao
Translated and edited by Mike O'Connor
160 pp, ISBN 0-86171-172-6, $15.95

The fullest translation to date of Chia Tao's poems, presented in both the original Chinese and O'Connor's beautiful English renderings.

"A gorgeous tapestry."—Anne Waldman, Naropa University

The Clouds Should Know Me By Now
Buddhist Poet Monks of China
Edited by Red Pine and Mike O'Connor
224 pp, ISBN 0-86171-143-2, $15.95

"A breathtaking anthology of Buddhist poet-monks, further enhanced by the original Chinese texts, plus excellent notes."
—*Inquiring Mind*

"Achingly beautiful poems. Highly recommended."—*Library Journal*